Crossed Pens

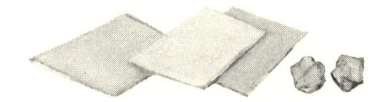

Crossed Pens
"A Gift of Laughter"

JAMIE F. MACVICAR

FREDERICK H. MACVICAR

PETER A. B. TAYLOR

ACROPOLIS

CROSSED PENS by Jamie F. MacVicar, Frederick H. MacVicar, Peter A.B. Taylor

Copyright © 1996 by Jamie F. MacVicar, Frederick H. MacVicar and Peter A.B. Taylor
All rights reserved

No portion of this book may be reproduced in any form without written permission from the publisher, Acropolis Books, Inc., 415 Wood Duck Drive, Sarasota, FL 34236.

If unavailable in local bookstores, additional copies may be purchased by writing to the Acropolis Customer Service Dept., (Phone 941-953-5214/FAX 941-366-0745).

Printed in the United States of America.

The Party's Over Now reprinted by permission of International Creative Management, Inc. Copyright © 1972 by John Gruen

FIRST EDITION

Library of Congress Cataloging-in-Publication Data

MacVicar, Jamie F. 1951–
    Crossed Pens: a gift of laughter / Jamie F. MacVicar, Frederick H. MacVicar, Peter A.B. Taylor
       p. cm.
    "The selected letters of Sir Jamie MacVicar, Frederick H. MacVicar (alleged sire), Peter A.B. Taylor (sculptuh emeritus!)"—Cover.
     ISBN 0-87491-974-6
    1. Man—Humor. 2. Fathers and sons—Humor. 3. Satire.
    I. MacVicar, Frederick H., 1928– . II. Taylor, Peter A.B., 1949– .
PN6231.M45M33   1995
816'.5408—dc20   95-26317
                                                                                     CIP

Author's Note

Dueling Pens, Swordsmen Three and *Hail to the Bon Vivants* all occurred to me as apt titles for the correspondence of three misguided and happily misspent men who have in common, above all else, loving to hear themselves write.

Whereas I take full credit for the idea of publishing these tender missives (with an occasional insight or two), I have done little editing other than to omit a line or two here and there that I deemed too personal, too confusing or just plain too pathetic. Other than that, the letters have been altered very little.

Whereas all letters have been to and from Jamie MacVicar, there are no letters from Fred MacVicar to Peter Taylor and vice versa. In fact, they at this writing have never met. Henceforth, as the gravitational center of this correspondence, I have duly elected myself editor-in-chief.

Fred MacVicar is my father (I think). Pete Taylor is my friend. Peter and I first met over ten years ago when he served unflinchingly as the art director for my then fledgling graphic design studio. He has since ended a life of structured employment to that of more leisurely (or at least independent) pursuits while sculpting in a studio nestled somewhere in the valleys of North Carolina.

A brief biographical sketch of each of us accompanies the editor's note to better aid our readers with our current activities, dilemmas and distinguished (if ill deserved and sordid) past.

In closing, as cads and bounders (speaking for myself, that is), incorrigible hedonists and keen observers of our fellow men and women, may we salute those who, tongue in cheek, find humor in everyday life, and may we honor those who honor us for our one (and perhaps only, some might say) stellar virtue... "To thine own self be true!"

Editor-in-Chief
Jamie F. MacVicar

Jamie MacVicar

Jamie MacVicar is the President and owner of a graphic design and communications firm in Washington, DC. Born in Fairbanks, Alaska to Canadian parents, he traveled throughout the south and attended three institutions of higher learning (all of which asked that they not be identified). He is currently writing a book, *The Advance Man,* about his three-year experience as an advertising man for Ringling Brothers and Barnum and Bailey Circus.

Fred MacVicar

Frederick H. MacVicar was born in New Brunswick, Canada. He served as an Infantry Company Commander during the Korean War (not in Korea, thank God!) and spent his career as an advertising executive in New York and throughout the deep south. A final stint for Her Majesty's Government included several years as Director of Marketing for the Smithsonian Institution Press. Currently, he resides on Hilton Head Island and owns a marketing research firm.

Peter A. B. Taylor

Peter Taylor was born in Wilmington, Delaware in the mid-twentieth century to a Belgian mother and an American father. After an idyllic childhood in pre-suburban environs of New Castle, Delaware, he earned a degree in Political Science at the University of Delaware and a Diploma in fine art from the Corcoran School of Art in Washington, DC. Armed with these credentials, he embarked on a career in art with enough detours to make even the most jaded traveler a mere tourist.

He is now a sculptor living in Greensboro, North Carolina with a wife of twenty-three years and a teenage daughter. When not courting the Muse, he works as Curator for the Greensboro Artists' League and practices the kazoo.

Contents

Part One

Tail Hoisting • Fruits de Mer • Royalty? • Sons • Transmogrification • Fountain of Youth • Sculpting and Selling • Under the Kilt • Cross Tabulations • Enlightenment

Part Two

Back on the Shelf • Roller Coasters and Merry Go-Rounds • The Island Fling • Passing the Torch • Dopey and the Nuns • Leering and Panting • Inner Growth • Lechery and Skullduggery • Parenthood...UGGGH! • A Fate Worse Than Death

Part Three

"Masculinity is as Beautiful in Its Own Way as Femininity is in Its" • Introspection • Fatherly Flagellation • Flagellation Unappreciated • Chippies and Chirpies • Spiritual Pleasures • The Birth of a Novel • Brothel Hopping • "Judge Not a Woman by the Depth of Her Cleavage" • Marriage • Lifeguards • A Novel Revisited • The Right to Bare Arms • Four Ingredients to Writing a Good Book • A Lover of Books • Charlie and the Reverse Feeding Method • Relaxing the Protuberance • Specialization and the Loss of the "Gentleman" • Head Mule Breeder • The Art of Sculpting • The Exotic Celtic Curmudgeons • Primogeniture • Asset Allocation • A Book of Letters

Part Four

"For Just as the Eyes Begin to Dim, We Begin to See..." • The Art of Disagreement • Honeymoons Remembered • "I Thought I'd Heard it All..." • A Religious Experience • Hawkers and Hucksters • Bottom Fishing • Forgiveness • Huck It! • "Wanting My Cake and Eating It Too" • Marriage Revisited • Spiritual Energy • The Life and Times of Peter A.B. Taylor • Memories • Fathers and Heroes • A Grain of Truth • Blending • Fathers and Sons

PART ONE

"Tail Hoisting"

TO JAMIE MACVICAR   FROM FRED MACVICAR   AUGUST 10, 1992

Dear Jamie, Spawn of the North,
   Sunday afternoon, while reading and tippling, I stumbled on a quotation by Mark Twain, to whit, "A man who carries a cat by the tail learns something he can learn in no other way."
   As you know, I have an inquiring mind and like to test the validity of such quotations. Accordingly, I lured my weird little cat, Stir Fry (whom you've met), within reach and hoisted her up by her tail. Never again will I question Mark Twain.
   While emitting bloodcurdling screams, flatulating in my face, and urinating all over me, she simultaneously inflicted more than two dozen claw marks on my once-handsome face, bit off my left ear, and barfed on my new boat shoes. It was awesome.
   Needless to say, I turned loose of her tail and dropped her. Apparently, the extreme stress of tail hoisting unbalanced her inbred, land-on-your-feet equilibrium, and she landed on her wee head, pissing her off something fierce. Although concussed, she managed to claw her way up my left leg and under my kilt in an all-out effort to emasculate me. I was doing my famous rendition of the highland fling in an attempt to dislodge her and remain a baritone. Just in time, her claws pulled loose from her toes, and she again dropped to the floor, this time on her posterior.
   We now regard each other with loathing, fear and unveiled hostility, both of us suffering from our wounds and taking painful rabies shots. Stir Fry never removes her World War II helmet nor wags her tail, and I never remove my cup.
   When Field Marshall Montgomery vowed he'd fight to the last drop of Canadian blood, he wasn't shitting. Nor was Mark Twain when he wrote that tail-hoisting a cat is educational.

   Love,
   Dad, the Almost Neutered Spawner of the North

To Jamie MacVicar   From Pete Taylor   October 14, 1992

Dear Jamie,

    Greetings and salutations. Here I am, clinging tenaciously (with liver spotted hands) to the first few days of my forty-third year. With aged dimmed eyes, I see the clouds of my life being swept and scattered by the Winds of Time—tossed and buffeted against this mountain of mortality. The relentless L'Eau de Realite cuts deeply, leaving me scarred with the lines of its passing. And yet, above this din, beyond the baleful drone of my lamentations and through the thinsulate of my L.L. Bean all-weather headgear, I still hear that sweet song of the Muse. She beckons to me now from the summit, just as she called to me when I was a callow lad bounding over the foothills of life. And so, once again, I resume my ascent. Spurred on by that vision on high—those twin orbs of Hope and Inspiration and that promise of the alluvial delta from whence cometh Truth and Artistic Realization.

    Hey, so I like to get reflective around some of life's little mile posts. Sort of a mental tune-up, oil change and front-end alignment. (I do wax automotive.) Anyway, I will soon be back to normal (a relative thing, what) and will try to subdue the voice of Capt. Jean Luc Piccard with its mental musings and Shakespearean soliloquies.

    As promised, a few pictures of villas (villi?) from the glorious South of France for your upcoming vacation to stimulate your visual input system and titillate your synaptics to the point of positive physical action culminating in the actual sensory experience of that magnificent, magical, Mediterranean marvel of Provence.

    Just to look at some of these villas, I am transported, suddenly ensconced poolside with a cafe au lait complete as the arcing Phoebes brightens the skies to a brilliant azure blue. Or, back from a vigorous hike in the hills (more likely a day misspent in leering at and lasciviously pursuing scantily clad, dark-eyed nymphets), I am ensconced on the terrace, tucking into a trencher of *fruits de mer,* crusty bread and enough of the local nectar to delight the palate and refresh the spirit. Oh, rapturous day! A veritable heaven for this lascivious hedonist.

But wait—time for a reality check. . .

I hope you find this info helpful—at least a starting point. You might also check your local library for ads in the travel magazines and other related pubs.

Until we meet again—take care. . .

As always,
Pete Taylor

To Peter Taylor   From Jamie MacVicar   December 14, 1992

My Dear Peter,

Once again you brighten my day with your melodious prose and wry, dry wit. Perhaps we may become pen pals, on the condition, should I run for political office, all mementos, thoughts, lewd observations and general reports of misconduct be sent to my Scottish ancestors for safe keeping and appreciation. I will, of course, do the same for you; however, having accumulated this knowledge over a lifetime, it would be a shame not to exchange our innermost thoughts, thereby leaving us with at least a clear conscience, since a clean one is out of the question. Who knows...men and our angst, women, spirituality, inner growth, peace of mind. Perhaps we'll even come up with an answer or two.

P.S. Since at this exact moment I am not engaged in the pursuit of money—my second favorite pastime—I wonder if I might trouble you to check our lineage. Is it possible two reprobates with a taste for the finer vices in life might indeed be descended from royalty? If not, it would be such a pity. Bullying innocent naifs being such a fine sport and all, but alas, I begin to ramble.

Thank you for the book on Provence. It was most kind of you, and if you'll loan me some of your better sculptures, I might pass myself off as a fine artist, thereby increasing my chances of La Linguas, at which point I will dispose of all future pretenses.

Well, do write soon, sharing any thoughts—original or stolen—and I will, of course, respond in same.

Best regards,
Sir Jamie MacVicar (Who's gonna check?)

To Jamie MacVicar   From Fred MacVicar   January 10, 1993

Dear Jamie,

Thank you for visiting. David's letter (enclosed) arrived right after you left. Hearing from both of my sons in a single year was a major breakthrough which I will treasure forever and enter in the family Bible for future generations and posterity.

I've been reading your manuscript and like it. I let three women read it over the weekend, and they all want to meet you at your earliest possible convenience. They don't like the circus shit, but think you might be interesting in bed. They promise to do their best to support our position.

The weather is lovely, Mary Jane extends her deep sympathy and best wishes, the economy sucks, the first debate was the pits, Atlanta lost but Toronto won and Elvis Presley was sighted on the beach yesterday. Other than that which never existed in the last place, let alone the first, all is concretized except that which is still very much up in the air—which is very much polluted.

Having brought you up to date, let's meet again sometime in the next century, at which time I will further enlighten you on the ultimate lessons of life.

As long as I'm writing this treasure of trivia, I'm also enclosing David's envelope, wherein he spells his father's name incorrectly and leaves off the Mr. and/or Sir—for which I want to be on record for forgiving him throughout eternity and thereafter.

Hope your vacation in the Virgin Islands was fruitful. As we know, most fruitful vacations take place in San Francisco, but "do your own thing." To me, if you see one fruit, you've seen them all. I prefer vegetables, like Bush and Clinton.

Sincerely, (wear condoms), yours, (finish your book), love, (family—not me—important), get a publisher, (soon),

Love,
Dad

To Jamie MacVicar   From Pete Taylor   January 24, 1993

Dear Jamie,

A heap of greetings and salutations be upon your fine self. How, pray tell, fare you in your myriad forms, both spiritual and physical?

Here I sit, at the start of the New Year, with your letter in hand and my schizophrenic synapses immediately undergo an epiphany which instantly illuminates that inexplicable and inextricable link that binds us, which is—or should I say are—the finer things in life. Those tangibles and intangibles that separate, if only by degree, man from beast. So, amid a few minor masterpieces, I ponder the fate of the civilized world as we know it and try to transcend it in a creative phasion. Imagine the burden, the awesome weight—lifting the whole of humankind to a higher plane of being. It just plumb tuckers me out sometimes, and I must take the pause that refreshes, nay, the rest that resuscitates. Double the reason (oh sweet reason) to enlighten you and to pontificate my latest ruminations.

I am at times much disturbed and dismayed by the global goings on, all of which leave me in a great, large fit of consternation. If events take many more barbaric turns, you may forward my post to the nearest industrialized, French-speaking city with cafes, indoor plumbing and long-legged women.

I shan't rail from my ivory soap box against any specific incident but with a force of will elevate my being to the lofty position of objective, non-partisan observation and thus, from this perch, ponder such objects of thought as: the social contract, personal responsibility, standards and achievements by which a society might be judged, inter-species dating, pluralism and the American political system, basic inadequacies of people who don't wear hats, government support of research and development, what's left if the religious right has its way, and Cindy Crawford, plus many other thoughts too numerous to mention.

As you know, it is time once again to conscientiously refrain from making any New Year's resolutions. Once again, I resolutely vow not to make any resolutions whatsoever. Some might say that people make resolutions to change some habit or behavior that they believe is detrimental to them. But I submit to you the real reason—it is more likely they believe what other people think will be, or should be, good for them. This, of course, is fallacious and detrimental to one's character development. As a young man, if following this line of reasoning, I foreswore my "misspent youth" as some might deign to call it, and "applied myself," I would have lost the foundation of true understanding of my fellow man—who when faced with moral turpitude gives in to wine, women and song. (I've sung that boozy lyric a time or two.)

And, herein lies the way to true understanding and the roots of compassion, "There, but for the grace of God, go I once again."

But, the trick is to maintain awareness of one's self throughout one's journey. Use the experience, not allow it to use you up. Constantly changing and reinventing yourself to the world until that outer self fits your inner self line for line and wrinkle for wrinkle.

What precipitated this particular digression was the idea of Sir Jamie MacVicar. Why not! We all manipulate our persona to the world. To some, it is a hairstyle or cologne (some imaginations can only manage an aftershave), but the truly creative and individual reinvent (discover!) their true selves. And what better vehicle than a nobleman with ancient celtic heritage, British style, plus humor and a touch of eccentricity thrown in. What a smashing opportunity!

Authentic British eccentricities—what a treasure trove, by Jove. A road, an autobahn to self actualization. Have you thought about wearing red Persian slippers embroidered with gold to complement a Saville Row suit and bowler? Affectations of speech: Hello, what's this? smashing, bugger it all! jolly good, dash it all. . . quoting the bard, Keats and Shelley, references to the teaming subcontinent. Construct your sentences with circuitous precision or specific ambiguity. . . but I shan't go on. Although this is a deep and swift stream of consciousness, I dare wet only my toes lest I be swept away by the current possibilities and battered upon the rocks of verbosity and end up in the eddies of endless digression.

Needless to say, some time has elapsed since pen was first set to paper. So without further ado, I shall brand this epistle forthwith and hasten the post.

Keep me apprised of your transmogrification.

As always,
Pete

To Peter Taylor   From Jamie MacVicar   February 1, 1993

Dear Pete,

As I read your latest correspondence and indulged in your stream of consciousness, "bouncing along the eddies" as you so eloquently put it, I could not help but think how wonderfully sublime (and odd, I might add) it is to have a friend such as yourself. A man that is able to defy conventional paths to prosperity (except for that minor interest you have in that massage parlor), take sculpting tools in hand, and devote one's life to the pursuit of one's art. Indeed, how many people could be so pure, so direct (by the way, are you still seeing that young model who posed naked for you?), so focused on such a noble mission that all other concerns should fall by the wayside.

But alas, enough of my praises. What about me, one might ask?

Well, strangely enough, a reporter has recently asked that question from the *Washington Business Journal*. They've apparently caught a whiff of my circus days, been pulled in by the lunacy of it all, and now wish to tell my story in two pages or less. I must say, I am certainly flattered, having been kicked through the goalposts of life by a series of bullies, low lifes and general miscreants yet survived thus far to, of course, deliver the same to others, but I seem to be digressing. The point of all this is that when one reaches one's forties, one begins to get a perspective on one's life. One begins to see how life's little twists and turns, hidden pathways and secret tunnels catapult one into a state of giddiness at one's present state or conversely into a sobbing, fist-pounding exaltation of life's wicked unfairness.

Fortunately, as I gaze about me, I find I am blessed to have found myself in the former state. How, might I ask, can this be? And then I realize that like you, my good friend, I have discovered the fountain of youth. That it is not plastic surgery, and that it is not chasing young women (I'm still testing this theory), but indeed it is continuously throwing one's self into brand new challenges, totally untested waters. For is the wonder of youth not the wonderment of the new?

Oh my, please excuse me. I simply meant to relate the news and instead have found myself rambling incoherently. So I will wish you a fair adieu and thank you again for your continued writings and valuable lessons. There are flurries of snow as I gaze out my window, Hillary has fat ankles, Jesse bit me, and Boris Yeltsin is going out with Princess Di. That's all the news I have.

Write soon. Your admirer,
Jamie

To Jamie MacVicar   From Pete Taylor   February 25, 1993

Dear Sir Jamie,
    Gad Zooks and Odds Bodkins laddie, what a dashing fellow on the frontis pagium of the local business rag. Bravo, you old scally wag, they even managed to spell the name correctly.
    It seems that you had the uncanny good fortune to avoid the January blizzard for a bit of dalliance in a warmer clime. Always one for a prudent and timely exit, preceded by careful planning and much consultation at the oracle, you managed to awaken my snowbound envy on that memorable weekend (the details of which I shall relate anon). No one can fault you on your timing, except that you missed a chance to attend the opening at Arnold and Porter. Your fine rakish self was missed, but carry on we did, and the show went well with three pieces sold, which lead to a third show here this summer and a commission for an outdoor piece. So all in all, things are as fine as frog hair, and I'm busier than a hooker at a Congressional Christmas party.
    Despite all the sawdust flying, I have been able to practice my culinary skills on out-of-town guests and not a few of the indigenous folk, none of whom is gastronomically challenged. To quote our much beloved ex V. P. , "A good waist is a terrible thing to mind." On this perplexing and awe-inspiring note, I must accept the onus of this truncated missive with the promise of a more expansive rumination to come. In the meantime, keep up the good work, and we'll see that devil-may-care visage of yours smiling at us from the cover of *Ad Age Magazine!*

    As always,
    Pete

To Jamie MacVicar   From Fred MacVicar   June 20, 1993

Dear Laddie Buck,

    On the occasion of my 43rd Father's Day, it occurred to me that I should write to my elder son. My grandfather always referred to me as Laddie Buck, because he couldn't keep track of his dozens of grandsons. Therefore, you are now the hereditary Laddie Buck. Wear this noble title like a crown.

    As I write, I'm listening to a tape entitled *Tilt O' The Kilt* which was donated to me by Sir Charlie Haggis, OBE, DSM, KC, PDQ and KP. I'm enclosing a copy of the tape, lest you forget.

    As you know, Sir Charlie, whom you met on your most recent visit, is Commander in Chief of the only Scottish regiment in South Carolina, and I am proud to serve under him as his Sergeant Major. The Hilton Head Highland Boozaliers is a very proud and infamous regiment with numerous battle scars and a reputation for capturing, holding and supporting watering holes in the Deep South States of the Scottish-Canadian North American Colonies.

    Sir Charlie has been temporarily posted to a remote outpost in New Jersey, where he is engaged in a life-and-death struggle with Croatians, Yankees and assorted street gangs. He was wounded twice in the left nostril last week, but being a staunch Scots-Canadian, has learned how to breathe through his navel and snort through his right ear. His tour of duty in New Jersey should end in September, and we're looking forward to his safe return.

    I'm delighted to know that you're learning to play the great highland bagpipe. As I told you in childhood, you have to blow mightily into your mouthpiece, let your little fingers roam over the holes in the chanter and squeeze the air out with your left armpit. The trick is to keep your bags under your sweaty left armpit. Personally, I like to change the bags every few months, since old bags tend to become irritable, expensive and somewhat "wheezy" after prolonged squeezing.

I'm sending Sir Charlie my one and only copy of your Profile article, in which you refer to me as a ski bum and Madison Avenue derelict. After reading this, Sir Charlie will undoubtedly reduce me to the rank of Lance Corporal and post me to front line duty in Bosnia-Herzegovina, where I will, as always, serve with distinction.

The *Journal* Profile article was very revealing to me. I had no idea that you were such a "Canny Scot." I only knew about the Tilt O' Your Kilt.

You've done me proud, Laddie Buck, and you're everything I always dreamed you'd be. Sir Charlie might approve of your enlistment in the Hilton Head Highland Boozaliers, providing you master the great highland bagpipe.

Please convey my love and regards to my only two MacVicar namesakes, both of whom, undoubtedly, have inherited their Grandfather's charm and talents. They are authorized to very proudly wear the tartans of both Clan MacNaughton and Clan Campbell, ad infinitum. I assume they're beautiful, like me!

The patron Saint of the MacVicar sect, incidentally, is Saint Dewar's White Label who discovered the best of the four major food groups and was a distinctly undistinguished leader of men, women and slaves. He ran dry on the Plains of Shorewood.

I think it's important that you know that there is only one authorized answer to the inevitable question, "What's worn under the Kilt?" The correct answer is, "To my knowledge, not a thing! To my certain knowledge, everything's as good as or better than new." If you're not sure, lie!

Well, Laddie Buck, it's unfortunate that you're growing old and crotchety, while I continue my youthful ways. However, a jet-set lifestyle, tycoonism and raunchiness will inevitably take its toll. Your mother was that way, as was your great-great-great grandfather, Kublai Khan, bless his soul.

Incidentally, you're not really my son. You were switched at birth by an inept hospital employee. Your real father is the head milker for a yak herd in Outer Mongolia. He'd like to visit you soon to introduce you to his 36 wives, one of whom is possibly your mother. He's not really sure. His name, should you be interested, is Yak Teet, and your real name is Muktuk P. Yak Teet the Great. The P. stands for Pygmalion. You also have 438 brothers and sisters, all of whom are anxious to spend some time with you in Washington and meet with the Great White Chief Tecumseh Clinton.

Well, Laddie Buck, keep your chin up and replace your old bags or your pipes will clog.

It's summertime here, and the birds are singing and doo-dooing all over my car. You'd love it. Stop by sometime and ask me how I rounded off your slanty little Mongolian eyeballs with two bamboo Swahili swizzle sticks. You'll love the procedure.

Peace be with thee, Laddie Buck. Although I'm not your true sire, I love you as one of my own, and you've "done me proud"!

Keep your powder dry, don't burn the haggis, never say die, don't shoot 'til you see the whites of their eyes, say your prayers and give thanks morning, noon and night.

Memorize the lyrics and melody of *Scotland the Brave,* hum it at work and just before your next libation. Always remember the immortal words of Coach Creol, who called you a slimy little bench-warmer of the First Degree, your first major recognition as a child. Also remember the endearing words of Kathy Brown's father when you ran over his new brick mailbox and the endearing words of your father when he saw the ass-end of his Dodge Dart convertible.

Your Most Esteemed Servant and Guidance Counselor,
Fred
Regimental-Sergeant Major "Dingo" MacVicar of the Long Lost Patrol
Regimental Headquarters, The Hilton Head Highland Boozaliers
Remember Our Noble Motto: "The Chosen Few for the Defense of the Brew"
Scotland's Canadian Defenders of the North American Frontier
"By Appointment of Her Rightful Majesty, Anne Boleyn"
CC Sir Charlie, Commander-in-Chief, OBE, KG, DSP, KC Knight of the Realm, Knight of the Garter, Nite-Nite, King of the Beasts, The Bull Goose, Head Curmudgeon, Icon.

To Jamie MacVicar   From Fred MacVicar   June 25, 1993

Dear Jamie,

Assuming you're still among the living, it occurred to me that you should be made aware of the unsurpassed services available to you and your clients which are economically and efficiently provided by MacVicar & Earley (no relation).

We have invested heavily in the custom tabulation and data analysis software that enables our computer to spit out every conceivable piece of data you might ever desire. With the proper amount of sniveling and whimpering, plus generous bribery, we can slant the information up, down or sideways. Everything is kept in complete confidence, of course, unless someone comes along who's willing to pay more than you, which (unfortunately for you) is almost inevitable.

This week, I re-examined the half-assed telephone survey you conducted for Union National Bank, in which I reluctantly participated and for which I was paid far too little and far too late. Upon review of that highly flawed effort wherein your stenographer and janitor conducted the interviews and you designed the crossword-puzzle, 1850-style questionnaire, I'm somewhat reluctant to offer our services. However, you are possibly my elder son, and I feel compelled to volunteer our services.

For your edification, I am enclosing a copy of the *Sporting Clays Magazine* questionnaire (page 80) along with the final tabulation of results. Also, I'm enclosing the most recent Visitor Survey tabulation we're doing for the Island Chamber of Commerce, along with a typical cross-tabulation, this one by "type of lodging."

We have an "almost unlimited" cross-tabulation capability in our system which will enable us to "break out" almost any of the demographic or psychographic categories you or your clients would need.

There's no way, Jose, that you can buy this kind of research capability in Washington for the unbelievably low prices we reluctantly charge our fortunate clients. However, in your case, after my last experience, I must insist on double the payment up front with the understanding that your alleged father will rebate 50% upon completion of the project.

Seriously, my alleged son, your alleged father and his very competent partner can perform any kind of marketing research your little heart desires. Furthermore, our involvement in marketing planning, strategy and management enables us to quickly point out your deficiencies when you are about to become a total A-hole in the planning and structuring of your pitifully inept "in-house" research efforts.

Try not to screw up a perfectly viable banking operation by creating misleading and unsubstantiated information. Let us do it for you at very affordable prices. We can show your banker how to gouge the living hell out of almost anyone with independently researched and carefully manipulated data which will stand up in any court in Outer Mongolia.

We can and do prepare written Agreements, but prefer to work closely and intimately with our clients on a handshake basis. In your case, we'd prefer to have a written Agreement with an iron-clad beneficiary clause in your life insurance.

It's been a joy to communicate with you, and I sincerely hope that they find a cure for your unusual, sexually transmitted disease.

I miss you, my alleged son, and hope to see you at least one more time before I depart this world. I'd like to deliver at least one more lecture on this earth before I help St. Peter get his act together at the pearly gates.

Affectionately yours, your alleged sire,

P.S. Thanks again for making me a ski bum instead of the respected commander of an infantry rifle company who was highly detested by everyone who served under his iron command.

P.P.S. Mary Jane, Boomer, Stir Fry and Quackers send you their gurgles, snorts, meows and quacks of esteem.

To Jamie MacVicar   From Pete Taylor   October 20, 1993

Greetings and best wishes you old froggiphile,
 Now that you have had time to re-acclimatize and re-culturalize, what do you think? Was Peter Mayles correct in chucking it all for the azure skies and red wine of the sunny south of France??? (Although I understand that he had an ancestral home and a few bucks in the Bank of Jolly Old England to fund his expatriation.) I can certainly see myself ensconced at the local cafe in ol' Provence, sucking up *une bonne verre* or two after a strenuous morning in the studio—girding up my artistic loins for an afternoon back at the atelier with the promise of a garlicky peasant repast once another masterpiece is wrestled into being to satisfy the ever-growing demands of collectors and museums the world over. There are a number of self-help gurus who posit the notion of visualization as an aid to realizing one's desires or goals. But as usual, being a small bore pseudo-intellectual, I am confused—should I visualize an ancestral manor with money in the bank, sunny Provence and me with a good red or collectors ringing my phone off the wall? As soon as I figure out this visualization thing, I'll beat cheeks to the nearest Air France office, and my next missive will be a carte postal from a place where even breakfast comes with wine and garlic.
 I can't tell you how happy I am that Fall has finally arrived. I love the Zen-like experience of raking leaves. I love the smell of wood smoke hanging on the frosty air and to hear the honking of the geese overhead (most honking is for slower geese to move to the back of the "V"). And, of course, FOOD, glorious food. All those marvelous dishes you don't cook in warm weather because it heats up the kitchen (and Mart won't allow me to turn up the air conditioning). Yeasty breads, simmering stews, roasting beasties, and last but not least, chili. There's nothing like a good dinner of chili and cornbread to bring one's thoughts back to hearth and home—to remind one of family and the need for good ventilation.

My daughter, Gisele, is now jumping two feet at the horse ring—quite the equestrian. Between school, riding and working at the barn on Saturdays, babysitting and some semblance of a social life (no dating yet, thank you very much), it seems that she is always going some place. I guess that's how it starts, first, weekends are full of activities, then a night or two a week, and then the next thing you know, you are waiting for them to come home from college at Thanksgiving to clean their room. . . why doesn't she ever bring the grandkids to visit?

I think this political correctness has gone a bit too far. There was an article in the local rag concerning costumes—the P.C. approach—no Indians, witches, drag queens, etc. Poor Gisele is in a fit of consternation. I'm all for social conscience and social responsibility with a good douse of civility thrown in, but give me a break—after all, a water buffalo is a water buffalo, and a good cigar is a smoke but not, of course, in an enclosed public space.

I have embarked upon yet another campaign in the ongoing quest for enlightenment and overall self-improvement. A never ending, and as some have said, impossible undertaking for me. Despite what my detractors would have me believe and with so much opportunity ahead, I signed up for a course offered at UNCG through the Emeritus Society. It was on Reason and Revolution. What better way to become enlightened than to take a course on the Enlightenment. I did feel a little dizzy several times during the class, but I attributed this enlightenment to the heady discussions or just from waking up in a strange place.

At the start of the journey, I struggled with the body/mind dichotomy. Where to start? To get the best results with the least amount of daily interruption and artistic down time, and not being able to do more than one thing at a time, I first had to decide the two important questions—is it healthy body, healthy mind or healthy mind, healthy body. As one can see, two of the great questions of our or any time that one can ponder. Even Hillary C. is probably musing on this very thing as I myself muse. Just think of it, two great intellects musing together on the same question—it does boggle one at times, but I'm getting used to it. Nevertheless, the question answered itself, as many things do if you just give them time and a certain distance.

The reoccurrence of an old back injury led me to choose the healthy mind, healthy body approach. Was it Fate, was it Karma, Divine intercession, who can say? I'll leave that bit of speculation to history and my biographers. My resolve having been fortified by this timely accident, I purchased a packet of motivational tapes—the basic premise being "choices." I am the sum total of the choices I have made up to this point in my life. If I don't like what I have made of myself and the position/situation that I am in, I have the options allowed by different choices to effect positive change in my life. One of the best ways to maximize positive change is to eliminate all things negative, negative thinking etc., etc. and so forth.

After listening to those six tapes while working in the studio, I was all fired up for positive change. In the words of that old chestnut, "accentuate the positive—eliminate the negative." This was all well and good until I came face to face with the possibility of a negative bank balance and the reality of a negative cash flow. Now this sounds more like economics, a subject that has put me to sleep since my college days. So I think I will author a self-help book on artistic expression, throw in a beret, black turtleneck and paste on my mustache and goatee. If I sell enough, this scheme will take care of my negative cash flow, negative bank balance and positively brighten my whole outlook on life. Then again, maybe this would be a bad choice, and I might end up losing money, alienating family and friends and I would be even further from enlightenment and more negative than ever. I think I'll go back and listen to that part about taking chances again. Or maybe I'll just wait until my back is better and try the healthy body, healthy mind approach.

Hark, I hear the song of the Muse and can see her nubile forms dancing around the studio, so I will bid y'all adieu and leave you with the words of the great one, blessings be upon his commercially available products and profits unto him who has the most televangelist stations, who said, "Rest not, nor be rooted to one spot on the path of life lest your soul become dusty." A-myn!

As always,
Pete

PART TWO

"Back On The Shelf"

To Peter Taylor   From Jamie MacVicar   December 12, 1993

My Dear Pete,

What a pleasure it was to hear from you last week. You brightened my otherwise drab day, as I contemplated the week following my forty-second birthday. These annual rites of passage can certainly be trying, as I cling to past joys (roguery all, ol' boy) and strategize an instant replay for the next twelve months. I told my friend from England I was now forty-two, and he simply paused and said, "Yes. . . you are getting on, aren't you?" Well, so much for the Brits. If it wasn't for us Americans, they'd have no one to make fun of, I always say.

Well, I'm back on the shelf. Yes, sad but true. Once again, another girlfriend bid a fond fondue. A bit troubling this one. The old ultimatum. She was a keeper though, so here I sit. Should I or shouldn't I. . . should I or shouldn't I. . . it's bloody maddening, but in a perverse way it's at least consuming, in a dangerous sort of way, that is. The other day I put the cat food in the refrigerator, the frozen food in the cupboard, and the cat in the microwave. I didn't know it, until after dinner, I was picking my teeth with a sharp object, looked down, and it was poor Muffy's paw. . . AAAGHH!

Business continues to go relatively well, and it's seldom boring trying to keep a crazed pack of Bohemians flying in the same direction. Fortunately, their eccentricities are far too divergent for any organized insurrections, so I remain installed as the Grand Pubaw for the foreseeable future.

My book continues to give me great satisfaction. I finished a major section last week and hope to fly to Indiana during the next month to lubricate my memory banks. Indiana was the scene of my demise, so I look forward to the trip with a well deserved trepidation. I'd elaborate, but what the hell, that's why I'm writing the book. Should you choose to sit back one day and find yourself staring at a published work with my byline, please know that, above all else, I was at least true to thine self. This won't save me from the shock and disdain of my old Sunday School teacher, along with a few other notables, but the elderly lechers will toast a drink (in a place, no doubt, where drinking socially is not allowed) with a hardy, "Here, here!" and that will bring a smile to me poor writer's heart.

Christmas will soon be here, and I wish you and your family the best of the holiday spirit. Please write again when the muse jumps from your brow, perches itself on your workbench, sticks its tummy out, and demands to be tickled.

    Your friend,
    Jamie

To Peter Taylor   From Jamie MacVicar   February 7, 1994

Dear Petah!

Thank goodness for your recent letter. As my thoughts during this wintry season drifted northwards, I pictured you either basking in the glow of a fire, warming your wool-clad feet on the stone hearth while your muscles are being gently kneaded by your charming wife and your thoughts reminisce (as great writers do) over the works of Wilde, Hardy and C. S. Lewis; or whether instead you were shivering between two cardboard layers, underneath the Tuscawanee Bridge, warming your hands to a Zippo lighter, having been tossed out for wild revelry, general roguering and a manly pursuit of libation.

Thank God, it's the former. People like you and me, having chosen the roller coaster over the merry-go-round, seldom have an in-between.

Life for me goes well—off to the islands in March to worship the sun gods and, hopefully, a trip to Ireland mid-summer. Business is good. Bob Lane wishes you warm regards. Hillary Clinton is secretly the Chief of Staff. And Senator Packwood was just elected to Head of Protocol. Other than that, Washington remains the same.

On a serious note, please let me know how the sculpting goes. Are you now simply designing and directing the work of others as in the olden days or hard at work from scratch to finish?

Thanks again for keeping me on your mailing list. I never take our friendship for granted.

Best regards,
Jamie

To Jamie MacVicar   From Fred MacVicar   February 8, 1994

Dear Jamie,

Since the marketing research business is trying at best, and Hilton Head Island is rather limited in size, I've begun exploring other options. In fact, Bunny MacNutt and I have decided to open a Scottish pub here on the Island. We plan to call it The Island Fling, specializing in Scottish cuisine, beverages and entertainment.

The bar and lounge will seat five hundred. The two dining rooms will each seat ten plus two high chairs for the bairns. The rooms will be wallpapered with both of our clan tartans, Campbell in the bar and MacNaughton in the dining rooms. The sound system will feature the pipes and drums of the Canadian Black Watch Regiment and the Glasgow Police Pipe Band. The around-the-clock entertainment will be provided by the gayly attired Highland Dancers of the Seaforth Highlanders, while a shirtless athlete tosses the caber around and about and curses in Gaelic.

Scottish sheepdogs will herd a small flock of mountain sheep through the dining rooms to entertain the chow hounds. The waitresses will be topless, wearing only their fur and leather sporans (to make change), along with their bearskin bonnets adorned with the MacVicar family crest. The barmaids will be similarly attired, but will carry their dirks in their stockings. The kilted sheep herder will carry a dog whistle and a scoop for the mountain sheep. In full highland regalia, I will lurk in the shadows overseeing the thievery of the employees and the excesses of the patrons. My partner, Bunny, will preside over the kitchen staff, eating her baked beans and thundering on the haggis.

Our breakfast menu will feature kippers, oatmeal, peat bog pie, tea and crumpets. Lunch will feature poached sheep's eyes, hardtack biscuits, pig's knuckles, feathered gull wings, oatmeal casserole and puppy dog stew. Dinner will feature bull tongue soup, thunder bunny haggis, salt herring, scones, boiled mutton, ground stag horn and Sassenach pudding.

The beverage specialties will range from little known meads and wines to the traditional Scottish brands. We will also offer discriminating topers a delightful choice of more exotic beverages, including Juice of the Loch Ness Monster, Shetland Pony Pisaller, Highland Dew Dew, Angus Dhu Dhu, Why Robbie Burns, Farewell to The Regiment, Thunder Bunny Bokay, Single Malt Vinegar and a Wee Dock and Doris.

Every other Sunday morning, we'll have a free mountain oyster roast before church services, and on the sixth Tuesday of every month, all drinks will be free. The Pope has agreed to give a Scots Presbyterian Mass in the Lounge every St. Andrew's Day, and Bill Clinton will tend bar on Veterans' Day. More than 300 hookers of Scottish ancestry have signed up to participate in our two-for-one happy hour festivities and a retired Pipe Major will play *Scotland The Brave* on his pipes whenever and wherever a bonny, fully-paid-up customer is flung from the Fling.

We open on the anniversary of the Battle of Culloden, and my partner and I are joined for battle with the Sassenach.

    Peace and Prosperity, Laddie Buck. Stay erect.
    Sire Frederick

P.S. There's a marvelous book out called *Passing the Torch*, should you ever wish to cash out and spend your final days as my chief chef and dishwasher.

To Fred MacVicar   From Jamie MacVicar   February 14, 1994

Dear Dad,

    As Luck would have it, a local Borders had a copy of *Passing the Torch,* which I have now purchased per your recommendation. I personally spend most of my time trying to grasp the torch (a wobbly, fumbly task at best), let alone figuring out how to pass it on once I've got it. But, nevertheless, the next time I'm wafting among the coral, contemplating this or that and either/or, I'll now have an excellent "how to" in which to navigate the shoals without crashing about the eddies.

    I look forward to our next visit, at which time I'll probably be humbly wondering how I ever had such gall to think beyond the week in the first place. Enjoy, and thanks for your ongoing wisdom.

    Best regards,
    Jamie

TO FRED MACVICAR   FROM JAMIE MACVICAR   FEBRUARY 24, 1994

Dear Fathuh!

How nice of you to send the book, *My Life in Writing,* by J. C. Furmas. I particularly liked the part wherein the author was ludicrously coaxed into the chess match with the Grand Master of Kiev, whereby three moves into the game, he accidentally extended his bishop one square too many, whereupon his Russian opponent stared at the board, stunned, shook his head and promptly resigned.

As a testament to your generosity, I have enclosed a tape of new age/Irish Celtic music by a group called Clannad. Although I've anticipated your response of "What in the world is new age/Irish Celtic music?" and "Has my young lad, my first-born son, so loved and admired (notwithstanding his moment of consummation following a three-day binge and occurring in a momentous flash between a belch and a deep snooze) turned into a commie, pinko-chasing lard of. . . etc., et al." At which I take considerable offense, and as a result, will no doubt extract my gift just seconds before sealing the envelope. Oh well, it was the thought that counted.

My book is now moving along at a healthy clip. I'm at the point where I've re-entered Indiana, the scene of my demise, which I now get to relive in minute detail. My reluctance to do so is countered by the fact that Indiana takes place in two cities with two sets of characters. This enables parallel plotting, which is fun to craft. . . cutting from one city to another, while leaving something of suspense for the reader to look forward to returning to.

I haven't submitted anything to the *Washington Business Journal* lately (actually the last item I submitted remains unpublished); however, I'm hoping my muse finds something soon to be outraged about. Unfortunately, outrage follows action, and all we've had in Washington for months is "hand wringing." Clinton to the Serbs: "If you bomb civilians one more time. . . well. . . well. . . I'll. . . I'll. . ."

Bomb explodes twenty seconds later—sixty-six civilians killed.

Clinton responds: "I've had it. . . do it one more time and see what happens!"

Gawd! One does wonder whether resolve was just a fad of the thirties. Surely Churchill would be turning over in his grave.

Well, enough of music, literature and politics. . . the point is (there's a point to this?) everything is constantly changing, yet nothing changes at all.

Thanks again for the book. Keep your mustache waxed, your wick dry and your knickers up. Take some names, kick some ass, and don't forget to snivel at the slightest threat of discomfort. . . it usually won't help, but everyone you know will be so disgusted you'll at least be left alone.

Take care and write soon.

Your loving son,
Sir Jamie
Heir to the Throne of The Isle of Hilton Head

P.S. Did you hear the joke about the seven dwarfs as told to me by an English friend?

> The seven dwarfs are gathered together and send Doc up to see Mother Superior. Doc knocks on the door and says, "Mother Superior, are there any dwarf nuns here in the convent?"
> "No," she says, "of course there are no dwarf nuns here in the convent."
> So Doc goes back down, and the other dwarfs ask, "What did she say?"
> "Well," Doc says, "she says there are no dwarf nuns in the convent."

"Well, ask her if there are any dwarf nuns in England," the seven dwarfs implore.

So Doc goes back up the hill and asks Mother Superior, "Are there any dwarf nuns in England?"

"No!" she says, "there are no dwarf nuns in England!"

"What did she say? What did she say?" the seven dwarfs ask again.

"Well," Doc says, "she said there are no dwarf nuns in England."

"Well, how about in the whole world? Go ask her if there are any dwarf nuns in the whole world."

So Doc goes back up the hill.

"Mother Superior, are there any dwarf nuns in the whole world?"

"Look," Mother Superior says, "There are no dwarf nuns, period. Not here. Not in England. Not on the whole planet. Have you got that straight?"

"What did she say? What did she say?" the seven dwarfs implore.

"She says there are no dwarf nuns. Not here. Not in England. Not on the whole planet."

Whereupon the seven dwarfs begin jumping up and down.

"Dopey fucked a penguin! Dopey fucked a penguin!"

To Fred MacVicar   From Jamie MacVicar   March 3, 1994

Dear Father,

In less than a fortnight (or it could be more, I haven't the foggiest idea what a fortnight is. . . but the word sounds great), I expect to be drifting lazily and aimlessly among the coral on a West Indies island, while my nubile companion runs naked through the forest with flowers in her hair bringing me nuts and berries, fresh fruit and other delights. "Why would a cad and a bounder such as I deserve such heavenly treats?" one might ask. And the answer is, I don't. That is, I don't deserve it. But I do appreciate it, and that's the difference between you and me, if I might so boldly venture forth. Whereas you always felt you deserved it (chest out, chin up, commanding presence, etc.), and as a result, you usually got it, you never did appreciate it. In fact, as I so often observed, the poor wee things usually ended up with a sharp kick in the rump to hasten their exit. Whereas, not only did I not think I deserved it (evidenced by my leering while panting yet soulful glances), when I did get it, my appreciation was unbounding. For days on end, I'd follow them about on all threes in a trance-like state of doleful appreciation, usually licking their face at every opportunity.

The reason I tell you this is, not only have I been a disappointment to others, but you can only imagine how disappointing I am to myself. Therefore, from this day forth, I have taken a pledge to follow in your footsteps, never again to be called a sniveling little bastard, but to stand proud, like my dear old dad, one foot on the bow of the boat, a cigar clenched between smiling teeth, while young women grasp my thighs, breathlessly grateful for my attention, while knowing, as you have known, "By George, I deserve it!" And, by damn, now that my father's sixty-five, I know he'd bloody well appreciate it!

My God, I'm sorry. Sometimes when I write, my subconscious takes over, and before you know it, I've rambled somewhat incoherently about thoughts that must have laid dormant in me for years. Some kind of Zen writing, I guess.

What I meant to say was, I leave for the Virgin Islands on Friday for what promises to be a nice week of R&R. My company turned a nice profit in February (an exception to this otherwise dreary winter's performance); so, I leave feeling as though I deserve a nice vacation, and I certainly intend to appreciate it, as I previously related in the utterings of my heretofore semi-conscious state.

Sorry to hear you're being dragged before the court of South Carolina to testify on the accuracy of a marketing research study you probably invented out of whole cloth. If you've any brains, you'll be sweating bullets at the thought of perjuring yourself, which you'll have to do early on to save your worthy skin. (How did you know they'd check to see if the sampling was real? Bloody bad luck, bugger all, rubbish, etc. et al). Therefore, I suggest you look the jury in the eye and state periodically with great sincerity, "I'm satisfied. I did what I came to do." With any luck, they'll either think you've transcended truth into a greater plane of consciousness, or they'll be so bewildered by the ridiculousness of the reply, you'll be forgiven for all transgressions.

Well, best of luck, and just remember, whatever happens, you didn't deserve it! Now, I'm confused.

Best of love,
Sir Jamie

P.S. A second thought is to wear your kilt, cross your legs demurely, smile sweetly at the judge, while repeatedly accidentally calling him by his first name. One of three things will happen:
1. You'll be thrown in jail for eternity.
2. He'll be so rattled, you'll be off the witness stand before you know it.
3. You'll have a date for Saturday night.

To Peter Taylor　　From Jamie MacVicar　　March 23, 1994

Dear Pete,

　　I just got back from British Virgin Gorda—another wonderful "travel experience." Note I have discarded the use of the word "vacation" in favor of "travel experience," thusly not only easing my conscience but rendering future trips an imperative (balance, inner growth, etc.); however, I'll fill you in in more detail at our next visit.

　　Business goes well. Am looking for a new proofreader. Not easy to find and we've won several awards this year. It's amazing how well people will do when you leave them alone.

　　Hope all is going well. Look forward to hearing from you soon.

　　Sincerely,
　　Jamie

To Jamie MacVicar   From Fred MacVicar   March 24, 1994

Greetings, my alleged elder son,

It was nice to hear from you this morning. Boomer, Mitzie and Stir Fry send their regards to my alleged elder son and his alleged siblings, et al. Mary Jane echoes their sentiments.

Having qualified as an expert witness in the fields of marketing and public opinion research before the Supreme Court of the State of South Carolina, I should like to express an expert opinion, to whit: There is no such thing as a Virgin Island. If there is, avoid it at all costs. Next year, visit the Nympho Islands just off the western coast of South Carolina.

I like your Irish tape. Your taste in music is improving. When I played that kind of music when you were a child, you'd stick your thumbs in your ears and vomit up your dog food. How times change. Then again, dog food is more palatable than it once was, and one's hearing deteriorates with age.

I will, of course, tell the tale of Dopey and the penguin in the pubs of Hilton Head, claiming (as usual) that this is my original creation. Never credit an Englishman, lest you anger Saint Andrew, patron saint of Scots. Also, never credit an alleged offspring, lest you anger Mother Superior.

Last night we had corned beef and cabbage for dinner in honor of St. Patrick, and today there's a foul wind blowing through the neighborhood. Cabbage does that to me, and I'm threatened with eviction and/or emasculation by the Xanadu Homeowners Association. It all depends on the wind shifts and my fellow man's compassion and understanding. I have faith in neither, but the cabbage will almost certainly weaken or lose its toxicity and, eventually, "pass."

Incidentally, with regard to my new "expert witness" status, I have informed the South Carolina Bar Association that I am also an expert in the fields of lechery and skullduggery. After presenting my credentials, they are convinced that I'm well qualified and would like to have you as an alternative.

We've invited Laura, Eddie and Matthew to visit for the Easter weekend and hope they can come. Haven't heard from anyone else in the clan. Talk to Billy Pike every week or two and try to keep his spirits up. He's pretty lonesome since Aunt Blanche died and with Uncle Bill in a nursing home. He's never really been alone before, and it's tough if you've never been in that situation. Basically, I've been alone all my life, and it's still tough sometimes to "cope" with periods of melancholy and discouragement. He'll have to do some mental adjusting.

Incidentally, before I sign off, there's nothing wrong with being a sniveling bastard, leering, panting nor licking faces if you don't overdo it. Everything in moderation. Also, I not only deserve it, but greatly appreciate it, now more than ever. And I no longer clench a cigar between my smiling teeth, I gum it. Besides which, I don't have a boat to stand proud on.

Keep well, Cad and Bounder.

Love,
Dad, aka Frederick The Great
aka Alleged Father of Little Lord Fauntleroy
aka Cabbage Fart Freddy
aka Dingaling Peckerwood Frederico
aka O Most Revered Alleged Sire

P.S. Kathy Brown's father just called and wants you to send him a check for his mailbox and the abortion. I told him the check is in the mail. Send me a check for the ass-end of my Dodge Dart convertible, plus forty years of mental anguish.

To Fred MacVicar   From Jamie MacVicar   March 29, 1994

Dear Father?

How pleasant to hear from you. I am glad you completed your day in the judicial system relatively unscathed other than a case of post traumatic shakes. Always damned dicey to be hauled before the unknown. . . never quite sure who you might have maliciously maligned in some previously cocky moment. Just your luck to have held the attention of local society at an annual banquet while bullying some fat little bastard into an unmerciful state of humility, only to find him two weeks later, black-robed and licking his chops, as you limp to the witness stand. Sobbing uncontrollably, while pleading how unthoughtful you'd been has been my modus operandi in similar circumstances.

I wrote all day on Saturday, from 9 a.m. to 5 p.m. Generally my brain goes south on me after three hours of hard writing, but in this case, I had two scenes inextricably entwined, and I slogged forward in fear I'd never again be able to reconstruct the details. Writing sporadically but with perseverance, I might add, plays hell with the narrative flow. I spend most of my energy figuring out where I am, so that by the time I'm ready with great aplomb to resume my discourse, I'm good for about one paragraph. In spite of myself, I think I'll be through in one more year, at least a solid first draft, at which time I'll probably discover, after four years, I have an unsalable monstrosity. If so, I'll take solace in my philosophy (feel free to steal this—I did) that it's better to fail at something worthwhile than to succeed at something that isn't. (If you think about this long enough, you'll go mad.)

My oldest daughter is off to Myrtle Beach with several of her father's dollars and a mischievous look in her eye. A little young for spring break, but she sold me into it. She's inherited her grandfather's sales ability ("He could charm a hungry dog off the top of a meat wagon," I used to tell her), so I caved in rather weakly.

My younger daughter is home, hopefully driving my ex-wife batty. One of my true luxuries in life is to call my kids and hear my ex in a state of apoplexy. I used to get them drums and sirens for Christmas and drop them off at her front door. I'd giggle for hours just picturing the wee hours of the morning.

– Two Weeks Later –

At 4 a.m. in the morning, one week ago, I received a call from the Myrtle Beach Police. Courtney had been in an accident. Despite a midnight curfew and supervision by a girlfriend's grandparents, she and two others snuck out in the middle of the night, only to end the evening in disaster. The driver apparently fell asleep at the wheel (Courtney was already asleep in the back), drifted to the other lane and hit a car head on. Courtney was the only one injured with a good-sized gash to the forehead and a severed nerve effecting movement of her right eyebrow. We retrieved her immediately from the hospital down there and with top-notch plastic surgeons at Children's Hospital in DC., got the nerve reconnected and the rest of the damage minimized. Needless to say. . . a hair-raising week. The sight of your pretty daughter being wheeled into an operating room is something I won't forget for a long time. But thanks to prompt and expert hands, she's on the mend, back at school, and if there's a silver lining, she may think twice in the future before putting herself in a dangerous situation.

Parenthood. . . UGGGGH!

Well, so long, amigo. Write soon. Fill me in on your latest adventures, misadventures and general psychic meanderings at your earliest convenience.

Love,
Jamie

To Peter Taylor   From Jamie MacVicar   April 22, 1994

Dear Peter,

How nice to see you last week. I was just sitting in my living room, gazing out my window, and thinking what an enjoyable chat we had. I don't know whether I have ever told you this, but I have a deck in my back yard which dips into a lovely, spring-fed lake and soaks up the afternoon sun. Every woman I have ever dated (of any consequence, that is) has looked at my deck longingly and giddily announced, "You must get a charcoal grill. What fun we can have." Whereupon I tremble in nervous revulsion. I have finally figured out why. It's my self identity. Can you picture Hemingway, Salinger, James or Wilde for that matter charcoaling for the neighbors? My God, no!

Sitting in Paris, Madrid, St. Tropez or along the banks of the Cote d' Azur at an outdoor cafe, legs crossed, cigarette poised and wine waiting to be sipped as the weight of the world is contemplated through world-weary, yet handsome, seductive eyes. Yes. That I can picture. But wandering through Hechingers in search of lighter fluid and hot dog buns. My God, no. Surely a fate worse than death. So you see, a simple request indeed, but alas, one my fellow writer can understand I must humbly decline.

But must we stop there. Heaven forbid, no. My list of iconoclasms include Little League coaching, carpooling, double-knit golfers (I never know whether to hit them or kiss them), vacation resorts with names like "Couples" and, of course, marriage unless entered into as a means to foreign entry or the age spread is thirty years. . . either way.

Lest one think I'm a bit of a snob, please note I find perfectly acceptable a constant state of horniness, tennis shoes with holes in the toes, handwritten manuscripts, dog-eared dictionaries, a two-day growth of beard, and a deep, rich tan.

I was delighted to see you last week; however, I was disappointed our time was so short. I was further distressed to hear there was a tiny, weeny bit of trouble on the domestic front.

When this sort of thing happens to a fine, moral family man such as yourself, I can only conclude the trouble with marriage today is a lack of brothels. Some might scoff at this notion, but back when a three-day binge of boozing and wenching was quite acceptable, there was no fifty-percent divorce rate. Take the mayor of my hometown back when I was a lad. He was a frail old chap, but it didn't stop him from frequenting Mabel's down the street. Word has it he liked to be encouraged with the back of a hairbrush while scampering about barking on all fours. Believe it or not, he was married for forty years. . . I rest my case.

It sounds like your sculptures are moving forward. Please send me some slides of your recent work if it poses no trouble. Fame and fortune are around the corner I am sure.

In closing, thanks for the visit. It was nice catching up, and I look forward to your future ruminations.

Jamie

P.S. Thank you for confiding in me about the sporadic yet too frequent episodes of "the black dog," or as the French say, "Le Depressione." Brothel hopping is also a cure for that as well; however, a listening ear can also be a good remedy. Impose at will!

P.P.S. Let me know if you'd like a visitor from the north or no'th, as you southerners say. The last time I was in the deep south, a herd of elephants I was leading dumped in front of City Hall, an act for which I have long forgiven the city.

PART THREE

*"Masculinity Is As Beautiful
In Its Own Way As Femininity Is In Its"*

To Jamie MacVicar   From Pete Taylor   June 8, 1994

Dear Jamie,

Greetings and salutations! Please excuse the tardiness with which this epistle arrives, but the Muse did beckon, and I to her most bounteous bosom had flown. She now seems to be on holiday, leaving me to my own devices and a life interspersed with other than artistic endeavors.

I too enjoyed our luncheon the other week. Too bad that time flies so quickly on such pleasant occasions. I can't tell you how much I appreciate the offer of your visit. So far, I have been able to keep the black dog at bay, but if it should bite, I just might call to see if schedules permit a visit one way or the other.

Your problem with the fairer sex and charred flesh a la deck should, I think, cause some alarm. I believe Freud would most certainly concur that you are treading on very thin ice indeed. It has been my experience, albeit limited, that the female is trying to appeal to your more primitive nature—primal urges if you will. Now there is absolutely nothing wrong with giving into one's primal side nor with the next action most likely to occur, that being much effort on the part of the female to engage in unbridled copulation in the natural environment. But subconsciously she envisions her fine self sitting cheek to jowl with you, huddled under a rock shelter, roasting a paleolithic joint over that ubiquitous fire, while several little neanderthals scamper about in fur nappies. There may even be a mother-in-law lurking in the back of the cave planning your nuptial bliss. So a word to the wise—CAUTION! ! ! my friend, in all things. Remember, when grilling or having a poke d'amour au natural, the world is full of wily women and poisonous plants, not to mention insidious and insufferable insects.

Enclosed, not only will you find a batch of slides, but also a copy of the painter Robert Motherwell's (another fine Scot) posthumous tribute to the sculptor David Smith. It reflects some of the same thoughts we discussed about male friendship and a certain level of understanding between men that I find difficult with most women. There are a number of reasons that come immediately to mind, the first three items on the list being sex. Obviously, what Motherwell is describing here is true friendship, a kind of male bonding, but it is not a quantum leap to the next question, that of the nature of a relationship with a woman. I hesitate to use the term ideal, since there is no such thing in a real relationship, and maybe that is part of it. That, with the sex matter out of the way, a man might be more accepting of a friend and less critical (less threatened or jealous and therefore with no need of lies or games). There is so much baggage that we carry around with us, from society and of our own making, that real relationships are difficult at best, no matter what the sex. Nevertheless, I thought you might find it interesting.

I better close this letter and post it before I lead that old black dog up to my butt and say, "Take a Great Bite." So, in the meantime—take care and keep in touch.

    As always,
    Pete

On David Smith

April 9, 1971

Considering the intimate scale of New York City's art community in the 1940s, and that both artists later acknowledged they had long before admired each other's work, it is surprising that Motherwell and David Smith did not meet sooner than they did. Although Smith had moved to upstate New York just months before Motherwell arrived in New York City in 1940, he frequently visited the city from Bolton Landing. And before their meeting in 1950, the two artists had corresponded with each other regarding Smith's contribution to Motherwell's magazine, *Possibilities*.

When Smith exhibited in New York in 1947, the Willard Gallery published three brief essays that he wrote for the accompanying catalog, two of which were later that year reprinted by Motherwell in *Possibilities*. At Smith's request, Marion Willard invited Motherwell to write a catalog statement for the sculptor's exhibit in 1950, after which the two artists arranged to meet in Manhattan at a bar on Forty-second Street.

Motherwell's marriage in 1958 to Helen Frankenthaler, for whom Smith felt considerable admiration and fondness, deepened a relationship among all three artists that was to end abruptly with Smith's fatal truck accident in 1965. Just months before, Motherwell had written a tribute to Smith, that was published in *Vogue*. Instead, it is Motherwell's moving account of his friendship with Smith, published in 1972 in John Gruen's *The Party's Over Now: Reminiscences of the Fifties—New York's Artists, Writers, Musicians, and their Friends* that is presented here.

On David Smith   April 9, 1971

I enjoyed David's companionship more completely than any artist I have ever known; he was a member of the family, with his own key to the house I have lived in on East Ninety-fourth Street for more than eighteen years (since the birth of my first daughter). I can still hear the key in the lock of the front door turn with warning, and his cheerful deep voice booming through the house with greetings, and under his arms wine, cognac, French cheeses, and once (memorably) a side of young bear that he had shot on his farm at Bolton Landing, Lake George. If it was late, he could be drunk, always cheerfully and perhaps abashedly—he was profoundly sensual, mad about very young women, but with a stern Midwestern puritan guilt (about working, too). Helen Frankenthaler and he and I would all embrace, and in the mornings she would have a beautiful breakfast on a hot tray and a flower for when he awoke, and he would be moved with tenderness after the roughness of his bachelor's life in the mountains upstate. He was the only man I was willing to start drinking with at a late breakfast, because it was joy, not despair.

I have had many close friends among New York artists over the years, but David Smith's openness—he was never on guard, except that he would not say anything against a fellow artist, because by having that life commitment, he was beyond reproach—only David's openness was matched to my own instincts. Moreover, he loved Helen, who had been one of his first patrons when, as a very young woman, she was going around with Clement Greenberg, and who never wavered in her belief in David, nor her open admiration for him ("open" is a very important word to me). With him alone among my close circle of colleagues would I talk about certain male things—

ON DAVID SMITH   APRIL 9, 1971

Mercedes-Benz (to which he converted me), shotguns, the wonders of Dunhill's tobacco shop, where the best dark bread and sweet butter was (Locke-Ober's in Boston), baroque music, Scotch tweeds, the pleasures and mysteries of Europe, the Plaza over the Chelsea Hotel (I converted him), the reminiscences of a Western American youth between two world wars, in short, his whole "Ernest Hemingway" side, so to speak, that was so adumbrated in New York City, and which, whether a fantasy or not, was a safety valve for both of us. Quite independently, we had come to roughly the same conclusions about aesthetic sources of our inspiration which, in ABC terms, might be put as any art before the fourth century B.C., cubism-cum-surrealism, James Joyce, Stravinsky, Picasso, the strength and sensuousness of materials themselves, and a certain "primitive" directness. There were of course minor blind spots on both sides: he liked to go to the Five Spot to hear Charlie Mingus or whoever might be there, while I've never been attracted to popular music, no matter how great; or once, when Helen and I spent a sleepless night at Bolton Landing, her anger at discovering our mattress was not on bed springs, but on boards. (When we visited him the weekend before his last weekend, he asked Helen what make of bed to get for us; and then ten days later he was dead. Ken Noland called us to come to the hospital at Albany, and we drove north at ninety-five miles an hour through the night to get there, but Tony Caro came out with his kind face and said David had died from head injuries a few minutes before. For some months afterward, when I would occasionally come home with two items from a shopping tour—say, sea salt from England for boiled beef—realized how deep my habit was to get one

ON DAVID SMITH　　　　　　　　　　　　APRIL 9, 1971

for him too. As always had he.)

David had many deep friendships, and I would guess with each that magic gift of making you feel you alone were the one. He'd been extremely handsome when young, and in his prime with his bear hugs and warm smile had the charisma of Clark Gable, or what a wonderful animal a man is, and how even more wonderful as a man.

On the occasion of his bringing the great hunk of bear meat, ghastly red (as much from the paprika marinade, I later realized, as from blood), it was the afternoon of a dinner party we were giving, and he would not have it that we did not serve the bear after the smoked Scotch salmon. Helen left us at the kitchen table (with a bottle of cognac before us) for a mysterious errand, and he and I ransacked a shelf of cookbooks for a recipe for bear. There was none, so we adapted one for roast venison, with salt, fresh pepper, bay leaf, burgundy, meat glaze, and at the end, ruby port and a tablespoon of red currant jelly for the sauce. (It was superb.) There were perhaps twelve of us at the table, high on Scotch and wine and animated conversation, and Helen brought in the bear on a large platter after clearing the first course, and sat down in the middle of an absorbing story by someone. Suddenly she said, "David, look at me!" and he burst into raucous laughter as we looked at her in an apron on a bear suit costume that she had rented at a theatrical supply house that afternoon and, as the little bear of the three bears, began to eat roast bear, like a cannibal, but a most ladylike one...

I first met David in 1950. Marion Willard, his dealer, had sounded me out as to whether I would write a preface for his forthcoming show, to which I agreed, and it was arranged that he and I, who had never met, though I had

On David Smith   April 9, 1971

admired his work for at least ten years before, after seeing an abstract steel Head of his in an outdoor show in Greenwich Village (he loved it that I remembered that head so well), would meet in a bar in Times Square around noon. After we met he said, "I'm drinking Irish whiskey with Guinness stout as a chaser." "Fine," I said (after all, I am a Celt), and we proceeded to try to drink each other under the table. By midnight we had not succeeded, I don't remember where we ate (at Dorothy Dehner's?). I do remember driving my jeep station wagon back through the moonlit night to East Hampton, having a last beer to sustain me at Smithtown (or was it the name?), and wondering, before I fell into bed in a stupor, how I had made it, good a driver as I was in those days. But it was in 1958, when I married Helen Frankenthaler, that we became a trio, a special dimension in all our lives.

His two daughters were almost the same age as mine, we both delighted in them, adored them in our clumsy way, and when he had his daughters on leave from their mother, I helped him "entertain" them. He loved during the summer to bring them down from Bolton Landing to visit us at the seashore in Provincetown, where I've mostly gone for the summers, and my daughters still remember their childish awe at him finding a wet, torn dollar bill in the outgoing tide. He and I both loved a menage, with women, children, and friends and a bountiful table and endless drink, and we could do it unselfconsciously with each other, which is perhaps the deepest relief one peer can give another.

And we both knew damned well the black abyss in each of us that the sun and the daughters' skin and the bounty and the drink could alleviate but not begin to fill, a

On David Smith   April 9, 1971

certain kind, I suppose, of puritanical bravado, of holding off the demons of guilt and depression that largely destroyed in one way or another the abstract expressionist generation, whose suffering and labor was to make it easier, but not realer, for the next generation. And if they liked it cool, we liked it warm, a warmth that is yet to reappear in the art of the young generations who have, as they should, their own life styles, whether chic or hippie or what. In any case, during the last year before he killed himself in his truck—his beautiful head was crushed against the cargo guardrail when he drove into a ditch, chasing Ken Noland in his English Lotus sports car to an opening at Bennington—David subtly changed, as though, about to be sixty, the old bravado was no longer self-sustaining. That optimism that we had shared through everything fluctuated ever so slightly, he made a will for the first time (naming me, without my knowing it, as one of his three trustees and executors, doubtless because of his daughters, his sole heirs); sometimes when very drunk he would begin to talk with a touch of paranoia about other artists or his domestic life, and sometimes despair would darken a moment. Then we would wordlessly pat each other on the shoulder, and have a final drink before bed. Rothko, in the fifties, before he himself began to drink a lot, used to say to me angrily, "Your solution to everything is another drink." Now I do not drink at all, they both are violently dead, Helen Frankenthaler and I are splitting, and I have invited David's daughters to visit with my daughters again this summer (1971) in Provincetown. I have felt deeply for various men during my life—masculinity is as beautiful in its own way as femininity is in its—but there will never be another David Smith.

| To Peter Taylor | From Jamie MacVicar | August 9, 1994 |

Dear Pete,

    First and foremost, allow me to acknowledge a fresher understanding (thanks to your last correspondence) of the many merits of charcoal grilling and secondly to extend my appreciation for the "Tribute to David Smith" you enclosed. As a sometimes reluctant but always immersed student of human relationships, it's gratifying to take a break from my ongoing angst of women versus men and rest my weary brow on the feelings of men towards men. As not only a randy but also a passionate and romantic sort, I seem to be forever wrestling with why what seemed so wonderful in so many ways in the beginning somehow in so many ways deteriorated in the end. For many, just grasping the emotional realities of the aftermath with all the direct sobbing and gnashing of teeth, not to mention the indirect kicking of the dog and picking barroom brawls is quite enough to eventually journey through the whys and why nots.

    Unfortunately for me, that is not enough. I must also "intellectually" understand what happened and why. This is especially true when I have walked away from that which many would greatly desire, but yet I cannot somehow incorporate into my soul. This process of course doubles the length of the journey, but on the same token, along with understanding, one grows, and along with growth, the future (at least when the past is repeated) becomes clearer. At any rate, I've now accumulated a fair share of highs and lows in relation to the fairer sex, and while licking my wounds, have written copiously on any and all insights along the way. It might be fun someday to do a book of short stories on relationships from the "male" perspective. Since most men don't analyze such things very much, they probably won't care to read about it either, but there may well be a market among women who could enjoy a deeper understanding of the male's conflicts and thinking. Sort of a male version of "Cowboys are my Weakness" by Pam Houston.

The summer has been a mixed bag. A nice trip to Cancun in June for a tour of the ruins, a Mexican bullfight, and a week of partying brought a welcome diversion. My book progresses along—a bit slower than I'd hoped this summer—my angst for a lost love is slowly abating despite a crooked path with a few sharp turns, and business is doing steadily well in spite of my lack of effort which has been stellar of late.

I am seeing a new woman, a warm, spontaneous and sexy creature with great depth and a still unjaded appreciation of the world. As of now, we are scheduled to spend a week in Bermuda beginning next Wednesday—a fine tribute to the summer's ebbing tide. My health has been an issue this summer for the first time in many a year. First a virus started with a body shaking, sopping fever which left me out of work for a week and exhausted for another. No sooner had I recovered, than my stomach erupted—probably from an overdose of antibiotics they gave me to cure the virus which then screwed up the bacteria in my digestive track. For the last week, it's felt like the Olympic Games have been sponsored by my lower abdomen. The gymnastics I could handle, but the javelin throwers have been murder. This too will pass.

Well, Pete, I have rambled enough but hope I've made some sense about a summer of love lost, love gained, travel, roguering and physical retribution. At the risk of sounding cloying, I sometimes feel I've chosen a strange life. One of intense pleasure and also great sorrow. A middle of the road would no doubt lessen both, but I don't think I could do it.

Write soon. Take care and keep well.

Your friend,
Jamie

To Jamie MacVicar   From Fred MacVicar   August 20, 1994

Bless you my child:

Hopefully, I've not ruined your Bermuda vacation with your newest chippie.

Two days ago, as Hurricane Chris was organizing some 1,200 miles SSE of the Leeward Islands, I purchased, heated and ate seven cans of Bush's Baked Beans. In an attempt to create a low pressure trough, thereby causing Hurricane Chris to veer to the North, I set out to fart it to a standstill.

The morning after I consumed the baked beans, I stood naked in the surf, aimed South by Southeast and expelled flatus at the rate of approximately 100 RPMs. The wind was out of the Northwest, which was ideal for my purposes. Unfortunately, midway through the Bush Bean Hurricane Protection Project, a wind shift occurred. An estimated 12,000 tourists evacuated the beach and left the Island. Rumors abound that a pod of sperm whales washed ashore and laid rotting on the beach in the hot August sun. Untrue.

In any event, my efforts proved fruitful, and Chris is now pointed towards Bermuda. Unfortunately, the local economy is suffering, and I was arrested by the Coast Guard who thought I washed ashore from Cuba or Haiti. On the plus side, I will be the new VP for Product Development for Bush's Baked Beans as of noon tomorrow.

Thanks for sending me so much information and the many fine photographs of my granddaughters, Courtney and Kristin. They will rank high among my many treasures.

Should Hurricane Chris approach Bermuda, I suggest that you consume a case of Bush's Baked Beans and fart downwind. If the wind shifts, catch the first flight out. Either way, it's a gas and you will live forever in the annals of Bermudian history.

Flatulence, when properly directed and controlled, wins wars.

Affectionately yours as always,
Daddykins
Your alleged progenitor and senior advisor

To Fred MacVicar   From Jamie MacVicar   August 26, 1994

Dear Father,

How can I respond? Standing naked in the surf, in a full fledged flatulent effort to ward off tropical, gale-force winds that might interruptus my coitus operandi. How many men can boast of such fatherly devotion?

Unfortunately, your efforts worked all too well. Every day I'd be coddling and nuzzling "my newest chippie," as you so elegantly put it, in the fevered and much awaited hopes of frenzied scissor locks, not to mention deep and tender caring, only to be met by her repose, "Oh, darling, it's much too nice a day. Just wait till the first rainy day. I swear we won't even get out of bed." Whereupon, the bubbly and, might I add, spry little bird would spring out of bed, donning motorcycle helmet and sexy European dress and race about the island with me in hot pursuit. Well, every day was more beautiful than the next, and by Wednesday, despite my feeble and sickening grin, I soon had the face of a recently smacked ass.

Well, you can just imagine the lift in my spirits when that evening I heard of the oncoming tropical storm. "For God's sake! This isn't just a rainy day, it's a damn typhoon!" I exclaimed to myself, whereupon I envisioned grappling and thrashing about only equaled by the crashing of waves and hurricane winds. "Yes!" I said to myself, "Yes! Bring on that mother!"

Of course, I was much more discreet to her, "Oh, dear," I'd say as I glanced up from the paper, "a bit of a storm headed our way. We'll certainly be stuck inside all day."

Well, you can only imagine, as she flitted about, how each day the storm approached, I became more and more excited. In fact, I could hardly contain myself when I awoke Sunday morning, perched naked on all fours at the foot of the bed and stared out the window in glee. Dark clouds. The blackest clouds I'd ever seen were approaching fast. My little chirpie moaned and stirred against her silk nightie. "Wake up!" I said. "Wake up!" no longer able to control myself, "It's here! By God. It's here!" Whereupon, inexplicably (until now, you son of a bitch!), the clouds suddenly stopped, reversed themselves and began tumbling backwards. "Come back," I sobbed, "come back!" as my little friend awakened and leaped out of bed.

So, as you can see, despite your best efforts, you did indeed ruin your poor son's vacation, for which you'll be forgiven only if you repeat the procedure redirecting the storm in this direction.

Your loving son,
Jamie

To Jamie MacVicar   From Fred MacVicar   September 1, 1994

Dear Son,

I'm delighted to learn that your Bermuda vacation was ruined while I sweated out the food stamp line on Hilton Head Island.

In your letter of August 26, much to my dismay, I detected a misconception on your part which requires clarification. Otherwise, you could be in deep doo doo or deadly peril.

In the second paragraph of your letter you referred to your companion as a "chippie" and in the next-to-last paragraph as a "little chirpie." Perhaps I should explain the difference:

A "chippie," in modern American slanguage, is a young, lust-laden, immoral female who ranks sex higher than immortality.

A "little chirpie," on the other hand, is a parakeet, canary, a small informer employed by the police or a diminutive cabaret singer.

It's possible to be both a chippie and a chirpie, in which case you can enjoy "Roll Out The Barrel" while you have sex, that is if she's a cabaret singer type chirpie. You can have sex on the wing if she's a parakeet, or kiss your ass goodbye if she works for the cops. Examine your options.

All of which reminds me. Should you run into either one, ask politely if they know the difference between mad, passionate sex and a tuna fish sandwich. Should they say no, promptly ask what they're doing for lunch.

It's nice to hear from you. Write soon for more fatherly advice.

Love, respect and sympathy,
Dad

To Peter Taylor   From Jamie MacVicar   September 3, 1994

Dear Peter,

It is the beginning of a lovely, three-day, Labor Day weekend, and I do hope you and the missus have a boodle of plans. I personally intend to get a little writing done, work in a little tennis, catch a movie or two, and reflect poetically on life in general.

Reflecting is something I've discovered I cannot not do. It's probably because I'm far more interested in "why" than "how," an artistic characteristic which leads to incessant gazing, not to mention considerable scratching. I bring this up in the face of a habit I discovered. Every evening, after coming home, I exit my front door, turn right, and proceed to walk slowly around the lake that sits comfortably in the middle of our little neighborhood. The wind usually provides a tranquil, rippling effect upon the water, and two or three families of ducks are usually, by now, swimming lazily home. Halfway around the lake, a park bench facing eastward peeks out between two shade trees, and offers a perfect view of the evening clouds and oncoming dusk. It's a spot I can't resist. In fact, it's so peaceful I often find I can barely move. Except, that is, for this aforementioned habit I've developed. The more I sit, and the more I reflect, the more I find my head slowly tilting toward the sky. As I become even deeper in thought, my jaw slowly opens, and I find myself at first pressing my tongue against the back of my front teeth and then, as I totally lose track of time and space, moving my tongue left to right and right to left. At this point, I am contemplating things that Kant, Descartes and Plato himself would be proud to discern, not realizing, of course, that, with the exception of drooling and rocking back and forth, I now look like the village idiot.

Fortunately, I discovered this slight little transgression (thanks to a small child pointing at me) and have now returned to a more stately composure while deep in thought. So then, what, might one ask, is the purpose of this revelation I have just shared?

The answer is twofold. First, to relate how fortunate I feel to be among those that daily appreciate and revel in the beauty that constantly surrounds us (we can, after all, ol' boy, choose to see the world as a beautiful place or as an ugly place and find plenty of evidence to support either view), while awestruck by the mystery of it all (when you think of how the world was viewed a thousand years ago and a thousand years before that and think of how we see it today with all of our knowledge and understanding, then it boggles the mind to wonder how it will be viewed a thousand years from now) and; secondly, to suggest, should you find yourself in a similar state, which I'm sure you will quite often, do try to look brighter than I.

Hope all is well. Write soon, and, as Henry Thoreau used to begin conversations with his close friends, "And what has become clear to you since the last time we spoke?"

Sir Jamie

To Fred MacVicar   From Jamie MacVicar   September 17, 1994

Dear Father,
  Thank you very much for pointing out the difference between a "chirpie" and a "chippie." It's quite clear good, solid, fatherly advice never ends. In fact, I'm reminded of the time when, as a young lad overly excited about something or other, you took me aside and said, "Son, did I ever tell you about the Papa Bull and the Baby Bull?"
  "No, Dad, you didn't," I replied.
  "Well, son, it's like this. One day, the Baby Bull and the Papa Bull were out walking, when suddenly they came over a rise, and there before them was a whole herd of cows. The Baby Bull got all excited, began jumping up and down, and shouted, 'Papa, Papa, let's run down there and get us one of them heifers!' Whereupon the Papa Bull slowly turned to the Baby Bull and said, 'Let's just take our time, stroll down there, and get *all* them heifers.'"
  So you see, years later I have you to thank for these little parables that have helped shape my passage into middle age, which, believe it or not, is a not-so-perfect-but-will-have-to-do segue into the purpose of this letter. I've been thinking about a few ideas for my next literary challenge following the completion of *The Advance Man,* which is now cranking along briskly. The reason for such thoughts is to avoid the deep funk that no doubt follows the completion of a lengthy piece of work.
  Since *The Advance Man* is light in several places and, I hope, entertaining throughout, it is nevertheless a dramatic and serious story. As a result, I thought it would be fun to embark on a journey that is educational but largely humorous in scope. In so doing, I've invented a character (with qualities only we could appreciate) by the name of Sir Harvey McDougal. Not unlike the "Flashman" character created by George McDonald Frazier, he's a cad, a coward and a bounder, bawdy to the bone, but through rotten luck and then uncanny wit, he gets thrown into situations

he desperately wants no part of but somehow comes out smelling like a rose. I plan to use real historical events and well known historical figures and then put McDougal into the middle of the fray. In this particular case, I've chosen the 1930s, where McDougal is reluctantly thrown between Hitler and Churchill as preparations for World War II rapidly unfold. In a few weeks, I'll scratch out the first few pages, which will show you the writing style I intend, as well as the dilemma McDougal has found himself in. Meanwhile, however, as Frazier did with *Flashman* and for that matter, Robert Graves did with *I, Claudius,* I plan to write the whole story but pretend I have only acted as an outside observer copiously taking notes and editing only slightly McDougal's recollection of events. To illustrate my point, I've written the introduction to the book as follows.

Editor's Note

It gives me great pleasure to present the first volume of memoirs of Sir Harvey McDougal, international statesman, military war hero, circus advance man, entrepreneur extraordinaire, and a host of other adventurous pursuits, not to mention recipient of numerous medals and a multitude of accolades, almost none of which were deserved, but all of which were gallantly received.

As the reader will note in Volume I, McDougal continuously finds himself in the midst of historical events and in close company with some of the most famous and notorious people of his time, from Adolf Hitler and Winston Churchill to Rudolf Hess and Albert Speer, not to mention numerous notables you'll recognize in this first recounting of his affairs. One might ask why a man of such prominent acquaintanceships in the midst of such momentous events should be hitherto unknown until the time of this writing. I too was baffled by the extent of Sir Harvey's anonymity until, through hours of intensive interviews, I realized that, at any one time, he was climbing down the drainpipe of life with his trousers in his hand, evading her majesty's taxes, an unknown number of offspring, ex-wives and ill humored compatriots. So despite a life of incredible achievement and worldly riches, a low profile and fleet of foot were his most precious assets.

But now, in the final decade of his life (or so he claims—the last time I saw him he was tap dancing with the nurses), he is anxious to relate the times and events of his checkered but fascinating past. With his extraordinary memory, I have mainly restricted myself to editing his comments for chronological order, punctuation and narrative flow. Much of his dialogue and many of his experiences no one can prove, but his accounts of historical events, both small and large, I have verified and found consistently accurate. Hence, I have no reason to doubt his other recountings. Besides that, although a handsome charmer, hopeless womanizer, cad and a bounder, not to mention coward and unmitigated social climber, the one creed he has lived by and repeated countless times during our sessions was that, above all, if nothing else—to thine own self be true.

Well, there you have it. As I indicated, I'll scratch out the first few pages of the book to see what you think. Write soon, and keep your knickers up.

Sir Jamie

To Jamie MacVicar   From Fred MacVicar   September 23, 1994

Dear Jamie Lad,

After long, agonizing weeks in intensive care, I've finally returned home, bedridden but gradually regaining my strength.

When I undertook the assignment to write "The Comprehensive Guide to the Brothels of Western Europe," I had no idea of the extent of the exhaustive research and backbreaking labor I'd have to endure. My research assistants dropped like flies, littering the highways and byways of Western Europe. I had to carry on alone, living on oysters and cheap table wine.

I've had numerous skin grafts on my knees and elbows, and my lower back has been completely rebuilt. My principal research instrument was damaged beyond repair and had to be replaced. Somewhere along the line, I ate a bad oyster and now live in diapers. Furthermore, I have grossly enlarged ears.

In order to gain complete cooperation in my research, I was forced to promise the subjects starring roles in American films and free housing when they arrived in the United States. I used your name, address and phone number, so you'll probably be hearing from them from time to time. Please place yourself at their disposal and treat them with kindness. Some of them are nuns and missionaries, so watch your language and bathe.

I should be up and about in a month or so. Meanwhile, Tally Ho!

Your poor exhausted Daddy

To Jamie MacVicar   From Pete Taylor   September 29, 1994

Dear Jamie,

Once again, I bid you hello!

What has become clear to me? It is clear that, from your last letter, the environs chez vous are idyllic, to say the least. As for reflection—tried it once. Was getting a bit narcissistic—which I soon put right with a quick glance in the inward pool and saw only a face a mother could love. Mom, alas, is long gone, and I am past caring (well, almost), not, mind you, to the attention to my person but to the effect it might have upon others whose criteria for intraspecies judgment is superficial and whose intellect is correspondingly shallow. (Not that occasionally my altitudenous thoughts aren't brought low by the sight of a well turned calf, one that's really nice. But these are just passing primal passions of only momentary duration and of no significant consequence whatsoever. For to quote the Bard II concerning judgment and physical attributes (Chapter 14, Verse XXIII): Verily, verily, I say unto you all, judge not a man by the size of his genitalia nor the strength of his body but rather the size of his intellect and the strength of his character, and judge not a woman by the expanse of her hips nor the depth of her cleavage but by the breadth of her vision and the depth of feeling in her heart.)

Which reminds me, you did not mention in your last letter your trip to that island paradise accompanied by your friend. K-pasta? Or should discretion deaden my curious mind and cause my hand to cease its cursive inquiry? Pray tell, what gives?

While you were down in summer climes, soaking up the rays and a few rum concoctions, yours truly was being reacquainted with the harsh realities of Washington, D.C. beltway traffic at 5:00 p.m. on a Friday. That great southward trickle of traffic—we were all heading in the same direction, but most of the "others" were obviously spurred on by more plebeian motives. (I try to be an egalitarian, but sometimes the Light of

Truth blinds lesser mortals, which in turn effects their judgment and, therefore, their driving.)

The work progresses well with a few more pieces sold. I also have four pieces on loan for the International Furniture Market that takes place in High Point twice a year. Seventy thousand buyers and interior designers from all over. I'm hoping the exposure will generate sales or commissions—time will....

I am also engaged in the pursuit of part-time employment. I have a lead on a curator's position with a local art group. There is also a position for a buyer of color seps. and printing. If worse comes to worse, my wee hands might be consumed with retail endeavors. K-sera, sera and goodnight, Doris Day.

The muse is running around bare-ass naked again, so I better get back to work. In the next letter, I'll fill you in on my Hungarian dinner guests and the state of my deciduous trees—stay tuned.

As always,
Pete

TO PETER TAYLOR   FROM JAMIE MACVICAR   OCTOBER 4, 1994

Dear Peter,

Ah, yes! The Bard II. How fortunate to recall such wisdom. I too remember the words of a philosopher who once said, "There's only two things you have to decide in life. Where you are going and who you are going with. And if you get the order mixed up, you're in deep shit." Or, if you prefer, as Martin Mull once said, "The next time I have the urge to get married, I'm just going to find a woman I don't like and buy her a house."

At the risk of sounding curmudgeony, marriage isn't all that bad. In fact, after the first three years, my wife became like a sister. Which wouldn't be so bad if you lived in West Virginia and/or you liked your sister, but bless her little pea picking heart, if she was anything, she was at least self deprecating. In fact, I'll never forget the time she told me, "You know, I'm just a country girl and, to be honest with you, not very bright, so what I've done is gone out and bought the smartest lawyer your money can buy. I'll see you in court, my little smidgins!"

Now I know I'm sounding jaded, but for the life of me, it's a strange arrangement. It's the only agreement one enters into in which not even a teensy, weensy, little legal document is signed, yet by the time you're through getting out of it, you have a stack of documents three inches thick. It makes you wonder how many people would do it in the first place.

"We'd like to get married."

"You would, would you? Well, I see no problem with that. We have a team of lawyers waiting for each of you with about a hundred pages of legal documents for you to sign. As soon as we take care of that, we can move right along."

None of which, I might add, has anything to do with my feelings of love. God knows I adore women, and the truth be known, I'm a one-woman man, but as I sit and contemplate my twelfth anniversary of bachelorhood, I must say, it's a far better thing to be there because you want to be than to be there because you have to be.

But what about "commitment," the opposite sex will no doubt rally, not to mention the need to raise little "ankle snappers." To which I have no easy answers. But, somewhere between "till death do us part" and "would you like to go on a rafting trip?," there must be a middle ground. One that focuses on the relationship, builds the foundations, and somehow blends the male and female psyches. For as long as the goal is for each to push the other to a less-than-natural state, then I suspect the divorce rate will remain at fifty percent.

What makes it more difficult is the rules of engagement have changed. At one time, not too many years ago, women needed a husband for economic support, and men needed a wife for sex. Neither is true anymore. As a result, what used to be ignored must now be moved to the forefront. Mutual space needs, intimacy, mutual respect, courtesy, emotional support, common interests and a host of other factors, all of which make marriage a marriage in the true sense of the word. None of which can be secured when the primary goal is to sign a contract. Indeed, that may occur, and I'll find no fault with those that do, but let it be the result of well built foundations, not the objective of well placed intentions.

Yikes! Pardon the sociological digressions, but what is the point of a letter than to reach beneath the surface and muddy up the water every now and then.

Hope all is well.

Affectionately yours,
Sir Jamie

To Jamie MacVicar   From Fred MacVicar   October 12, 1994

Dear Little Boy Blue (that's what my mom used to call me),

Nana would have been 85 today, but she left us.

Yesterday was one of trial and tribulation, but I survived. I went swimming, and a riptide swept me out to sea. I was going down for the third time when the lifeguard grabbed me around my swan-like neck with his brawny arm and started towing me to shore. His name was Bruce, and he wears earrings.

He started whispering comforting words in my ear and asked me to vomit up as much seawater as possible, which I did. I felt secure and happy for the next hundred yards or so.

We were about a mile from the beach when a sea gull flew over and plopped droppings on my eyeballs. This gave me blurred vision and a stinging sensation, making me vomit some more.

Feeling very much better, I scanned the horizon and observed a three-foot-high shark fin approaching rapidly from our rear. I immediately had a stress attack and threw up again. When I regained my strength, I calmly told Bruce about the fin approaching from astern, whereupon he upchucked his lunch all over my upper torso.

Being a professional lifeguard, Bruce immediately analyzed the problem and whispered our only three options in my water-logged ear, to whit:

Option 1: Let him turn me loose and float face downward in the hope that the shark would mistake me for a submarine, and he could make it to shore to bring help while it circled me.

Option 2: Keep on as we were and let the shark nibble off little pieces of me, beginning with my toes, in the hope that we could reach shore before it reached my groin area.

Option 3: Fondle my lifeguard. Bruce gently assured me that he could double his speed if he were properly fondled. I threw up again, and he whispered that puking is a typical reaction to this option. I immediately felt better.

Decisions, decisions, decisions...
Bless you, and may an everlasting piece be with you.

Big Boy Blue

To Fred MacVicar From Jamie MacVicar November 10, 1994

Dear Father,

What a sight for poor old Bruce, coughing and wheezing and flailing about with your kilt floating about your ears and your spindly little legs going for all they're worth. (Not that your legs are spindly, it just might appear that way from a distance.) Thank God, at least you were in America. No dilly dallying around here, ol' boy. Imagine if you were home amongst the Brits.

"Bernice, my dear, is that ol' Fred out there?"
"Why, yes, I do believe it is."
"He's behaving kind of curiously, wouldn't you say?"
"Is he?"
"Yes, I believe he is."
"Well, poor fellow. Something must be done."
"Should it?"
"Of course it should. We are civilized, you know."
"Are we?"

(Note, the Brits always answer a declarative statement with a question requiring you to repeat yourself endlessly.)

"Well, of course we are. Except for, perhaps, ol' Fred out there."
"Really?"
"Yes, indeed. Quite morally undeveloped, poor chap."
"Is he?"
"Been roguering his cook for years, not to mention his chambermaid and his son's Sunday School teacher. It's a wonder he's the energy to swim at all."
"How frightful."
"Yes, yes it is."

By now, of course, you'd have been quite waterlogged, and they'd still be tapping their pipes, but if there's anyone who can talk themselves into trouble, it's the Brits. Which brings me to the purpose of this letter, which is the first few pages (per my promise) of your namesake, "Sir Harvey McDougal."

The book's narrative is done in first person, the story begins in London in 1930, and our protagonist, Sir Harvey McDougal (cad and bounder that he is), is up to his ears in trouble before he knows it.

Sir Harvey McDougal

Chapter 1

If it hadn't been for my unrestrained boasting to Tommy Raglan and a room full of lads slobbering at the bar, I never would have gotten myself into this pickle, and a damned serious pickle it was, I might add, especially since I now found myself professing undying loyalty to my old chum, Adolf Hitler, who was half crazed then and damned near foaming at the mouth now, and Winston Churchill (Winnie, to the lads), who was equally as mad, if for no other reason, he'd been forced to the back bench for the last several years. Which one craved power more than the other was frankly beyond me, and under most circumstances, I couldn't care less, but to the extent I was now in the thick of international intrigue, not to mention mortal danger, I had little choice but to play the cards I was dealt. And in hindsight, if I'd played them right that night at Finnegan's, I'd be drinking fine port and cocking my leg over the Colonel's shapely wife instead of listening to the ravings of an ex-German Corporal and wondering how to escape his clutches with my limbs still intact.

Frankly, as soon as Tommy Raglan began egging me on, I should have smelled a rat. He never liked me in the first place nor forgiven me for pinning his ears back in front of the regiment, but the sherry had lightened my wits, and I didn't see what was coming.

"Harvey, you must, you simply must regale the lads with your experiences with young Adolf," he said with a misty look in his eyes.

"There's really nothing to tell," I said feigning modesty to the onlookers.

"Of course there is," Tommy added. "Tell us how you befriended young Adolf and helped his struggling art career."

"Yes, do tell," one of the lads cried out.

I could see the boys were now anxious to glow in my worldly travels, so I ventured forth with how I met Adolf in Vienna. The year was 1924. It was shortly after World War I, and Hitler was pursuing a career as an artist. Each day, he spent hours drawing buildings and street scenes, but even though a spark of talent existed, he had no skills for people, and they all looked like stick figures. Nor could he accurately render the proper depth or perspective. Nevertheless, Hitler passionately pursued his craft and sought admittance into the Vienna School of Art and was mortified at their constant rejections. And it seemed, the more his art was rejected, the more he began railing against the Jews and burghers that brightened the city with wealth and well being, especially as his own conditions for survival deteriorated. Not knowing his political leanings, I saw him one afternoon rendering a full-scale drawing of a downtown office building. Leaning over his shoulder, I commented on his excellent choice of colors. At first, he ignored me, but unused to praise, he soon began to further seek my opinions. With a love of commercial art, I indicated his talent was wasted as a painter, and what he should concentrate on instead was architecture.

As our banterings continued on a daily basis, it became clear to me he was outraged over the reparations from World War I imposed by the Versailles Treaty and thought it was the Jews who had caused Germany's surrender. I soon realized he wasn't operating with a full "palette of colors," so I began seeing less and less of him, but not before he said, "Someday I will need great artistic vision, and I will call on you."

"So that, my lads, is the last I saw of Adolf Hitler. Now drink up," I said and ordered another round of drinks.

"Well, you're in great luck, as is Great Britain," Tommy Raglan said to me, as the boys listened eagerly.

I had already returned to some serious leching, as the barmaid rested her ample bosom on the railing, and I said, half listening, "How so, old boy?"

"Well, it just so happens," Tommy says with a glint in his eye, "the British underground has picked up the fact Herr Hitler is in the midst of trying to find a symbol for his new movement, a logo if you will."

"Well, bully for him," says I, as I winked lasciviously at the barmaid who was now reading my thoughts.

"No, bully for you, old boy!" Raglan said. "As luck would have it, I've reported your acquaintanceship to British Intelligence, and they've requested your presence at 0900 in the morning."

"What in God's name for?" I said, trying to sound stoic but sensing the dithering fool had found a way to wipe the grin off my face.

"Well, I haven't the faintest idea, but I'm sure they've found a way to use your service to advance Her Majesty's royal mission," Raglan announced.

To hell with Her Majesty's royal mission, thinks I. Every time Her Majesty has a mission, better men than I, less skilled in fleeing for cover, end up dirtying their britches. Whatever Hitler was doing over in Germany, it was the last boiling pot I wished to be in. Damned be to Raglan. I'll get him for this.

"Yes, yes, a fine show," I said, as I raised my glass. "Whatever I can do for Her Majesty's Secret Service, I look forward to with enthusiasm!"

* * * * *

There ends the first few pages of Sir Harvey McDougal. In the next scene, the Colonel of British Intelligence (whose wife McDougal had planned to mount) informs him he's to become a part of Hitler's inner circle, while Churchill himself wants first-hand knowledge of all his exploits. Wanting no part of Hitler and his ruthless gang of thugs, McDougal does his best to wiggle a fast retreat, only to be informed, "It would be a shame if a few past tax indiscretions came to light." Meanwhile, as McDougal prepares to leave, Raglan begins eyeing Harvey's shapely fiance, whose only response is a batting of her lashes. All in all, "the whole damned mess is enough to churn your stomach," as McDougal would say.

Well, Dad, there you have it. Whether an audience exists for a dastardly rogue amidst a fascinating historical period is frankly beyond me, but it would certainly be fun to write, and "amusing oneself" is the first ingredient to good writing. At any rate, *The Advance Man* is still keeping me busy with probably a year to go to completion, so McDougal will have to sit on a back burner.

Hope all is well. Write soon.

Love,
Jamie

P.S. Any past anecdotes will certainly be appreciated. Mine will only last me a third of the way into the book.

P.S.S. You still owe me 50 cents (which, with interest, has now compounded to $7.52) for smiling sweetly while you told Dear Old Mum you got those scratches on your back wrestling with me on the floor.

P.S.S.S. Send a certified check.

P.S.S.S.S. Just kidding. A regular check will do.

To Jamie MacVicar   From Fred MacVicar   December 9, 1994

Dear Alleged Son, The Honorable Jamie P.P. MacVicar,

I haven't heard from you in many moons, leading me to believe that you are in your annual snit or deceased. Either way, I need to know so that I can make the proper entry in the family Bible. If in a snit, write. If deceased, communicate with me Sunday through your personal guru or psychic.

The women of Hilton Head are up in arms about the movement to amend the Constitution, revoking their right to bare arms. So are the beach boys and lifeguards. The thought of wearing long sleeves is abhorrent to their lifestyles. Long sleeved string bikinis are not in vogue here. The beach boys have uncontrolled diarrhea at the thought of having pumped tons of iron into hidden biceps. Their parents have devoted years to try to dissuade them from baring their tops and bottoms, and the movement has caught them completely off guard. They fear the next Washington ploy will forbid the baring of souls, the baring of ill tidings and the baring of illegitimate children. The poor bastards.

What in the name of Hell is going on in Washington? Are you in control or has Newt Gingrich driven you into exile? Are there any Americans serving in public office anymore? Which NASA scientist cloned your politicians and bureaucrats with creatures from outer space? Are you still dating Hillary or have you returned to the loving arms of Mrs. Bobbitt? Bring me up to date. Can you get the hell out of Washington?

Charlie and I enjoyed a crumpet yesterday, which we were forced to wash down with a quart of Dewar's White Label, while we listened to a tape of Harry Lauder and watched the shrimp boats scouring the oceans for prey. Charlie's in intensive care but is expected to recover with only minor brain damage. Major brain damage would require a major brain.

Write soon.

        Your Alleged Sire   Enclosure: Empty Dewar's bottle

To Peter Taylor   From Jamie MacVicar   December 10, 1994

Dear Peter,

Halloween has passed, as has Thanksgiving, as has my forty-third birthday since the last time we spoke. So what has become even clearer to me, one might ask. Well, I'm glad you did. What has become clearer to me, having just lost a staring match with my manuscript, is that there are four ingredients to writing a good book. These are now quite evident and once they have been accepted, one might, and I emphasize the word "might," succeed. The four, in order of necessity, are as follows:

- First, one has to have something to say. Now, since the size of a respectable book is four-hundred pages, and the average word length per page is three-hundred-and-fifty words, then one must be prepared to unburden oneself in approximately one-hundred-and-forty-thousand words.

- Having determined one does indeed have something to say and needs one-hundred-and-forty-thousand words to say it, one must secondly master the craft of writing it ...entertainingly!

- Thirdly, one must have the guts to say it. Putting down your true, raw, undiluted feelings, faults and foibles for others to read is harder than it seems. And the writer's mission is, above all else, to find truth, at least his or her own.

- Fourth and finally, one must be prepared to spend five years or more doing it. After all, writing a book is like making a fine wine. It takes time to age.

If still undaunted by the nature of "high thinking" versus the thrills of "high living," as Oscar Wilde said in *De Profundis*, then let no door, nor moat, nor obstacle be too great to stop the thundering herd of first-time novelists. (Which reminds me, how many books must one write to introduce oneself as a "novelist" without feeling incredibly silly? Was Margaret Mitchell a novelist? She only wrote one book. Or is Harry Snodgrass a novelist? He's written a dozen books, none of them any good, and none of them ever heard of. Or is the sobriquet "writer" a more appropriate term. Was Margaret Mitchell a "writer"? Somehow it seems a little understated. I mean, she wasn't exactly writing cereal boxes in between chapters of *Gone with the Wind*.) But I digress. Back to "high thinking" vs. "high living." I must confess, I agree with Hemingway, who said there is no point in writing until you're at least forty, since you simply haven't lived enough, (Dickens would disagree. Would you believe the bloody bastard was only 26 when he wrote *Oliver Twist*?) and that it is not a case of either/or, but for best results, a blending of the two.

Well, at any rate, as you can see, some things have become clearer, while others have become muddier, but more importantly, how art the world of sculpting? Many a writer has sputtered and spewed his innermost thoughts on the craft of writing, but rarely (in fact, never) have I heard the thoughts of a sculptor on the craft of sculpting. Perhaps in your next missive, you might ruminate a bit on your work.

Christmas draws near. The weather is balmy, and I hope all is well.

> Your friend,
> Lord Jamie
> (I decided I deserved a promotion.)

To Fred MacVicar   From Jamie MacVicar   December 11, 1994

Dear Dad,

I have not disappeared. In fact, the other day I was perusing through a few things you left behind many years ago and stumbled upon a book, *The Collected Poems of Robert Service,* you at one time owned. He was a Scotsman and a Canadian like you and a traveler like me. But at any rate, there was one small poem that I particularly liked. So much so, I had the first verse framed and placed in an appropriate spot.

> BOOKSHELF
> *I like to think that when I fall*
> *A raindrop in Death's shoreless sea,*
> *This shelf of books along the wall,*
> *Beside my bed, will mourn for me.*

Robert Service

Love,
Jamie

To Jamie MacVicar   From Fred MacVicar   December 18, 1994

Dear Alleged Offspring,

Thank you for responding. This week has been one of great trials and tribulation, and it's not over yet. Both my psychic and I are stressed out.

Four days ago—it seems like years—my pal Charlie, whom you've met, had another terrible accident. His condition could best be described as "suspended." Early Tuesday morning, wearing only his kilt, he carried his trash to his fourth floor trash room and while dumping it down the chute was goosed by an intoxicated college student who mistook poor old Charlie for the dean's wife.

Somewhat startled, to say the least, poor Charlie lunged forward and plunged headfirst down the trash chute, dropping like a rock before he got hung up on his protuberance somewhere between the second and third floors. Trashed by a mighty goose, he whines, snivels and whimpers incessantly, driving the other tenants to the brink of madness. They want to put him to sleep.

I've been pumping soup and scotch up to him through my garden hose, but the law of gravity prevents him from swallowing it properly, him hanging upside down like that. Tomorrow, I'll try feeding him from the other end with the aid of a plumber's helper lashed to a thirty-foot bamboo pole while pumping up toilet tissue from the lower end of the chute through a six-inch diameter section of sewer pipe I found in the town dump. He seems to be somewhat reluctant to experiment with my reverse feeding theory, but he's intrigued by the concept and the possibility that he will be making medical history, brave lad.

The Emergency Medical Service specialist in trash chute crises has patiently explained to Charlie and me that his only hope for survival is to somehow relax the protuberance that has hung him so high and dry. Charlie, now in his 80s, says that he'd rather die than relax his protuberance, and I tend to agree. A staunch protuberance is hard to come by, in great demand and important to one's self esteem. I've told him to hang onto it, but he says he can't reach it in his present cramped quarters.

The Swiss government flew in a crack avalanche rescue team Thursday and lowered their best St. Bernard down the trash chute. Unfortunately, the oversized mutt became enamored with poor Charlie's posterior and has no desire to re-position him, let alone fetch him or relax his problematic protuberance.

Charlie's been hanging upside down for four days now and frankly, I'm nearly at my wit's end. His 90-proof blood supply has accumulated in his brain pan, and his ears ring when we pipe his favorite melody, "Lurching through the Rye," up the trash chute, courtesy of The Gay Sanitation Workers' Kiltie Band. Tomorrow, I plan to read him "Ode to a Mighty Goose" by Robbie Burns.

In a MacNutshell, I need help. The pipers are weary of piping, the tenants are weary of Charlie's moaning and groaning, the garbage collectors can't use their trash chute, and the poor St. Bernard's exhausted. Can you help?

Affectionately yours, your alleged progenitor,
Father

To Fred MacVicar   From Jamie MacVicar   December 20, 1994

Dear Father,

It has become clear to me that your attention to poor Charlie Haggis is deserving of nothing less than the Victorian Cross. Unfortunately, in your single-minded devotion, you have been fixated on the symptoms rather than the cure. The heart of the issue, as you so delicately put it, is the relaxation of the protuberance.

Might I suggest:
I.   A prolonged conversation with my ex-wife's attorneys,
II. A visit by Rex Reed and his friends, or, if all else fails,
III. Free tickets to a week-long cruise with Joan Rivers.

If that doesn't send him down the chute, nothing will.

Glad I could help.
Sir Jamie

To Fred MacVicar   From Jamie MacVicar   December 21, 1994

Dear Father,

Specialization! I'd like to proffer it's killing modern civilization. Not in the sense of technological advancement. My God, we have laser surgery, high-speed computers, supersonic transportation and hundreds of other things that have made our lives easier, but, sadly for modern man in an extremely important way, specialization has not brought progress. In fact, I'd argue in one sense of the word the opposite has occurred. Along with specialization, the "gentleman," the "man of letters" has all but disappeared. Now don't get me wrong. My idea of a "gentleman" is not some trust-fund baby, but rather the likes of a Rhett Butler, a self-made man of derring-do who was just as comfortable among men as he was with the ladies of Belle's bordello, but, nevertheless, he was a man of refinements and broad interests and, consequently, deeper appreciations.

Perhaps it was his era. Everything prior to the twentieth century was much more elaborate—architecture, fashion, art, language, music, style of writing, furniture, bric-a-brac, etiquette, even the art of conversation. In fact, there were people invited to dinner parties simply because of their reputation as "great conversationalists." Sadly, a friend of mine, a fellow at a local university, told me the other day that, in five years, he has yet to meet a fellow faculty member that can broach three subjects in one conversation. And this is a liberal arts institution!

So what has brought this on? What cataclysmic events have led to the extinction of the "gentleman"? My friend says it was World War I. Prior to World War I, Europe reveled in an appreciation of beauty, refinement and worldly pursuits. But the devastation, slaughter and carnage brought on by World War I was so shocking that a world of refinement came crashing to its knees. Perhaps it was the invention of the automobile. Along with transportation, the world took on a faster pace. No need to linger days at a time with friends because it took so long to get there. And perhaps it was television. The chief form of entertainment was no longer books and other people. And perhaps, more than anything else, it is "specialization." Perhaps people have spent their lives mastering one or two crafts and have neither the "time" nor the "inclination" to broaden their interests and appreciation. So, as a whole, man has progressed. My God, we've progressed. Never has so much been accomplished in so short a time. But as an individual, my God, have we declined.

Broadening one's interests is a lifetime achievement. Fortunately, the task is sweetened by its addictive rewards. But somewhere along the line, one has to start. And as I reflect back on growing up, I remember your appreciation for art and music, history and commerce, dialogue and debate, sailing and the manly pursuit of worldly adventure. As a result, I'll probably never be a "gentleman" in the "old sense" of the world, for our era no longer puts a premium on such values, but I will continue to have a rich inner life and endless appreciation for a broad array of subjects, and for that I thank you. For, as I reflect on life's more delectable desserts, these are the things that I most appreciate. Merry Christmas. I love you.

Sir Jamie

P.S. To show I'm not living in the past, here's a futuristic prediction. As we move closer and closer toward on-line CD-ROM information at our fingertips (multi media though it may be) and farther away from the interactive lingering quality of books, the situation I describe will only worsen, thereby leaving a smaller and smaller conglomerate of in-depth, cross-linking inter-disciplinary thinkers.

Well, who cares, one might venture forth. No one, if the motive is profit, for just as Ford discovered that the separation of function via assembly line production is more profitable, then so too has our economy in a technical age discovered specialization of knowledge is more efficient to the whole. However, if one's motive is spiritual, not economic, then the development of human potential is a grave concern indeed.

To Jamie MacVicar   From Fred MacVicar   December 23, 1994

Dear Jamie,

I just received your letter on "specialization." Speaking of which, I just got fired from my job as tambourine player for the Hilton Head Island Regiment of the Salvation Army. The Colonel caught me with my hand in the kettle and had me stripped of my rank and drummed out of the Regiment—a dastardly deed for which I promise revenge. He'll rue the day he snatched my beautiful tambourine and $8.45 out of my sweaty little hands.

On the other hand, my Daddy always said, "A change is as good as a rest." The tambourine was beginning to rattle my nerves, and the kettle was far too tempting for a man of my tender persuasions. Accordingly, I've taken a management position I really enjoy on a big, one-acre South Carolina mule ranch. These are purebred racing mules valued at almost $10 apiece. There is one Jack (bull) in the herd and 68 Jennys (cows), and I was initially employed as Head Mule Breeder.

Helping the Jack off and on the Jennys 68 times a day hurt my back. He weighs almost 2,000 pounds. He was easy to get on, but I had to fight him to get him off. We were both tired of the work, so I asked to be reassigned as Head Mule Skinner. He only sired one alleged calf, which looked amazingly like this bull moose which has been grazing and mooing in the pastures.

The very first day on my new job, the Jack caught me sneaking up on him with my shiny new butcher knife and kicked me through the barn door, fracturing several ribs. Knowing my limitations, I immediately applied for the job of mule shoer and have been shoeing all 69 mules ever since.

Shoeing 69 mules is not an easy job, but I've got in-depth experience in shoeing my alleged children and female acquaintances. Accordingly, career-wise, I think I've hit the Jackpot (or Jennypot).

If things go well, I expect to be promoted to Head Jenny Milker early next year. Having heard the rumor, the Jack is making eyes at me and sending me posies. Unfortunately, I believe he's impotent, he's overweight, and he smells like doo doo.

Speaking of doo doo, would you be interested in marketing an unlimited supply of mule-doo to Nigerian farmers for a 2.3% of the gross. Also, what would you charge me to package it?

Respondez Sil Vous Plait.

P.S. I'll soon have my BS in Animal Husbandry.

To Jamie MacVicar   From Pete Taylor   December 24, 1994

Dear Jamie,

Greetings and Salutations! Yes, yes, it is official. I have found gainful employment as a curator for the Greensboro Artists' League. I've been busy scheduling the coming year's exhibitions, since the last curator left things hanging a bit.

Ruminate you say! Now there is a scary thought. Obviously, you have never sat around a kitchen table in the shank of the night with a couple of artists and watched as a bottle of Jack eased the tongues of the assembled.

For me, the decision to be an artist was never a conscious one. Although I spent most of my youth avoiding conscious decisions if not consciousness itself. Nor did it have anything to do with the prospects of nude models despite the fact that sex and sexuality have always been elements in my work. The conscious decision was to attend art school after earning a degree in political science and then at a later date to arrange my time to allow me to devote most of my energies to making art. During all this time I made art in one form or another. Even as a rosy cheeked lad, I enjoyed drawing and making things with my hands—toys, carvings and whittled objects.

Then, in my early teens I began to realize that I was reacting to certain works of art in ways that I did not fully understand. There was a world of beauty, power, sensuality, horror and mystery, all those terrible and wonderful things, that I felt plugged into.

It was at this point that I wanted to be able to make things (objects, drawings, etc.) that could express my own similar feelings, thoughts, questions and reactions—not to be an "artist" but to make objects that had meaning for me. Eventually, and on the practical side, I wanted other people to be affected by my work and buy it so that I could make more work!

Over the intervening years the work has gone from two dimensional pieces focusing on the female figure to assorted three dimensional abstract pieces in bronze, wood and mixed media. Though outwardly the work has changed, there are aspects of the work that have remained constant. I too am more three dimensional now and prefer a mix of media.

As for my thoughts on my own sculpture in particular? Being somewhat cynical and leery of artistic pronouncements, I will say that the work deals with issues of beauty, balance, tension, sex, certain formal aspects of composition and juxtapositioning of elements that I personally find interesting and is a cure for warts and manic depression.

"I make art; therefore, I am." Having said that, I now dispense with the intellectual aspects of my work!

On a more serious note, I do derive great satisfaction from the process of object making on physical, spiritual and emotional levels. In fact, there is nothing that supplies the same feelings of sustained satisfaction for me.

I endeavor to make objects that elicit an emotional response from the viewer. Just as one reads a poem, a novel or looks at a painting, he or she relates to it on several levels, filtering it through his or her experiences, testing it against his or her own framework of beliefs and references, accepting, rejecting, interpreting, changing, feeling—and so forth. When making my art, I operate from my own system of references but there are always things that appear in the work that I have no idea where they came from and I like it like that.

I'm now gearing up my digestive juices for the coming feasting season.

I'll write again as soon as I replace fork with pen.

Enjoy your holiday and best wishes for a happy and healthy New Year!

As always,
Pete

To Jamie MacVicar   From Fred MacVicar   January 10, 1995

Dear Laddie Buck,

It's a new year, and I've embarked on an exciting new venture with my bonny auld buddies Charlie, Angus, Dingus and Snort. We've formed a new troupe of folk dancers billed as The Exotic Celtic Curmudgeons.

Our agent has us booked for 500 one-night stands in taverns, pubs and bawdy houses throughout Central America, Australia, Borneo and Outer Mongolia with side trips to Tibet and Java.

I do the highland fling, Charlie does the sword dance, Angus does the sailor's hornpipe, Dingus does the Irish jig, and old Snort does the lurch, stagger and reel—all to the skirling of the great highland bagpipe. It's pomp, stomp and ceremony.

Our joints all crack in time with the music, and we sound like bowls of Rice Krispies, snapping, crackling and popping in perfect harmony. Thank God we're all on Medicare. I bruise up a lot clicking my heels together in the highland fling, Charlie whittles his toes in the sword dance, Angus gets mal de mer doing his hornpipe, Dingus has fallen arches from doing his Irish jig, and Snort loses control of his swagger, lurch and reel, often colliding with bung starters, floors, walls and cell doors.

Well, we're off to El Salvador in the morning, where we'll be house guests of Rosa Lopez while performing at the El Prostituta. Do you think we'd look nice in pink fluorescent hightop Nikes?

Love and gestures from the twinkle toes whom the highlands flung.

To Fred MacVicar   From Jamie MacVicar   January 22, 1995

Dear Dad,

Just think, you could have been a beagle. I call your attention to the plight of poor Fred as revealed to me in a newspaper story I clipped from the *Washington Post* the other morning.

> ...ded to Cuba.
> ■ New York police Sgt. Hector Collazo, 36, was stripped of his gun and badge after being implicated in the death of Fred the beagle, a department mascot who apparently relieved himself in the station house. After finding Fred's droppings in the station weight room Dec. 10, officers allegedly beat him, dumped him in the trunk of a patrol car and took him to an animal shelter as a stray. The shelter put Fred to death three days later.
> From news services

Let's face it, Fred, life's unpredictable, which brings me to the topic of this letter. The laws of primogeniture. Now, according to this ancient tradition, as the "Eldest Son," and allow me to put this as delicately as possible, upon your death, amidst the grieving and wailing of close friends, relatives, ex-wives and ungrateful siblings, as your property is tallied, examined and analyzed for all to hear, I, being your eldest son (and I put this as simply as possible), get it "all."

Now I know this sounds a bit harsh, and some would even say "unjust," but I merely am following the guidelines established by our forefathers. Having established my "rights," as they say, my question is, exactly what does "all" entail? Perhaps, and I must say I'm a bit embarrassed to ask, you could list your assets in the notebook I've attached. Feel free to use the back of the pages. Now don't get me wrong. I personally hope you live at least another 30 years, but a life of leisure, especially in this modern age, is not easy to plan; hence, my request.

Your Loving ^Eldest^ Son,
Lord Jamie

To Jamie MacVicar   From Fred MacVicar   February 1, 1995

A Memorandum to Jamie P.P. Ferdinand MacVicar, Alleged Eldest Son:

Jamie P.P. Laddie Buck:
   I received your tender missive the other day requesting a list of my assets for your safekeeping; however, as I rapidly approach my unwelcome demise, probably within the next thirty or forty years, I find myself in need of the adventure, travel and challenges of which my mundane life has somehow deprived me. Accordingly, this will be my itinerary unless a storm blows me off course.
   I leave tomorrow on the whaling ship "USS Blubber," whereon I will serve as Ordinary Seaman and Ship's Bartender for a period of seven years, hunting humpbacks and sperms in the seas south of Antarctica. I'm paid ten percent of the blubber.
   When the whaling voyage is over, in 2001, I will transfer to a ten-foot dingy captained by an equally ancient Australian by the name of Dingo who will row me across the Pacific to the island of Tibet, where I will finally climb the highest of all of the mountains in the world.
   I intend to camp on Everest for three years (about 2004), shack up with the Abominable Snowman's youngest daughter, and then travel by kayak through the Gobi Desert in search of the Lost Ark. This will require an estimated five years, taking me to approximately 2009, A.D.
   After these travels, I will probably be somewhat less vigorous and will retire and write my memoirs. I have not yet decided upon the exact retirement location but think it will probably be in a peaceful setting such as Beirut, Sarajevo, Mogadishu, Harlem or Washington, D.C. As you know, I hate violence and pain.
   From time to time, I'll send you a note in an empty bottle, addressed to The Shores of Bangladesh, attention Jamie P.P. I

have to scurry off now to board the Blubber and serve up a nice hot toddy for the captain and crew. Hike up your kilt when wading all puddles.

Your loving alleged sire, whom you rightfully worship and admire beyond belief, as should be the case (24 bottles),

   Archbishop Frederick

P.S. Following all this, should I have any assets left, I assure you I will forward them to you posthaste.

To Fred MacVicar   From Jamie MacVicar   March 2, 1995
and Peter Taylor

Dear Father and Peter,

Unbeknownst to each of you, the other exists. In fact, over the past three years, I have been corresponding to each of you. And, true to my Scottish ancestry, I have been hoarding (saving if you will) the letters I have written and received. Well, not only have I amused myself in the process, but, indeed, I've been tickled (and enlightened) as well. Perhaps, the thought occurred to me (being not only a "sniveling" little bastard but a "greedy" one as well), others might be amused as well.

Inspired by such thoughts, I commissioned one of my artists to illustrate a cover and typeset the letters into book form. Enclosed is a packet for each of you for your perusal. As can be seen, I have not selected a title for the book (I lean on your help), nor have I written the Editor's Note (I've elected myself Editor-in-Chief, since neither of you are to be trusted in this matter), which will provide an explanation for this compilation of manly humor, insights and lewd observations. Also, page two could be a short bio on each of us with current occupation, past history, etc., written in colorful style. The bios are necessary for readership understanding, as our letters refer to our crafts and present activities. Although, Father, I might very well know far more about you than I'd like to, if you and Peter would both give me a colorful history (including present activities), it would be most appreciated.

Incidentally, the rule inside around the text represents actual trim size; however, it is much more efficient at this time to keep the manuscript 8-1/2 x 11.

I happen to think a market exists for a book such as this if properly promoted, both domestically and abroad. Hence, I proffer a three-way split minus any costs I might incur (not to exceed five-hundred-thousand dollars) to typeset, cover illustrate, and market the books to publishers and agents. Perhaps, Father, a man of your marketing savvy would have a few hundred ideas.

At any rate, just think, if we sell 1,000 books in each of 300 cities, we'll be splitting one million dollars in royalties, enough to make you piss on the drapes in glee.

Well, it's just an idea, one I'm better able to appreciate since I've been collecting all the letters. Should I never hear from either of you again, I'll assume it has no merit. Otherwise, "write away," my fellow swordsmen. After all, nothing ventured, nothing gained.

Your collaborator, corroborator or something like that,

Lord Jamie

PART FOUR

*"For Just As The Eyes Begin To Dim,
We Begin To See ..."*

To Jamie MacVicar   From Pete Taylor   March 14, 1995

Dear Lord Jamie,

 Greetings and salutations from one who is contrite and most heartily sorry for the length of time that has elapsed since I last put finger to keyboard. So I send belated birthday greetings, wish you the best of post holiday cheer and hope that you enjoyed a pleasant MLK Day.

 Having received your packet and cover illustration, I'm assuming that you survived the holidays none the worse for wear. I was surprised to see how poorly my typist performed her duties. She has been thoroughly chastised (a comely wench, she has been chased though not altogether chaste) and made to note the corrections to the epistles in question which I will be sending to you directly. Your typist, on the other hand, will be beset upon by a horde of ancestral specters descending from across the Pale to exact vengeance for the grave misdeed of inserting a "D" for my middle initial instead of the correct and most distinguished middle initials, A.B.

 I now know from whence springeth forth your warped sense of humor. As you know, I am not a "joiner," and I find uniforms rather unimaginative dress but, having said that, I would not mind hanging around with Fred and the Boozaliers—as long as they have room for a single malt man.

 Your comments concerning age and writing are, I think, for the most part true; however, the idea of self expression minus the notion of experience raises the curious question of young musical geniuses. From the existence of such phenomenons, one may conclude that the very young are capable of tremendous range and depth of feeling that some might find disconcerting. But, the age of forty seems about right for those with a little more than a spare tire under their belt and a literary bend to wax eloquent before they wane. For just when the eyes begin to dim a bit, we really start to see. And as the body does not respond as quickly or as forcefully as it once did, we realize that the pleasures of the flesh are but side paths on the road to true understanding. Also, just when you feel that you have run out of gas, you become flatulent. Funny how Nature has its way of compensating, isn't it?

I'm sure I told you that I am now counted among the gainfully employed, having taken a position with our local Artists' League. You may address me as His Employeedness, Curator and Exhibitions Coordinator. (Not to be confused with a curate of the ecclesiastical persuasion nor an exhibitionist of any persuasion.) It has been two months, and they haven't fired me yet. Fortunately they did not call you for a reference, or I might have had to take that position back at Chez Lulu's House of Feminine Charm and Video Emporium—keeping an eye on the likes of you.

At least now that I am paying my fair share to Uncle Sam and his illegit nephews, I certainly am looking forward to that big middle class tax break that they have been carrotizing for so long. On the rolls and off the dole. Speaking of Dole, I never trusted that fellow, but now that Newt is Speaker of the Free World, Dole doesn't look so bad. Gees, there is another one for the Relativists. Where I come from, a newt is a small salamander, a few of which are poisonous. I don't know if one can draw anything from this observation, but I'm always cautious when turning over rocks or beneficial government programs.

My Muse has been complaining of neglect. I can't blame her. She has been calling, but I have been distracted and a bit lazy (dare I admit to that) and have let her languish, lips pouting and those perfect orbs heaving with restless sighs. We did have a go-round yesterday, but when you have been away for awhile, it is like making love to a different woman. It takes awhile to get acquainted, so to speak. Being a sociable fellow and always up for the task, I told her that I would be more attentive and solicitous. She seemed pleased and vowed to be as familiar as my own thoughts.

In my constant attempts for self actualization and self improvement, I have started attending the local choral society. Adding my own mellifluousness to that esteemed organization. It has been quite satisfying and should hold me until the lead for *The King and I* or *Kismet* opens up. In the meantime, I'll be content to be a bathroom baritone. My neighbor was saying just the other day that it sounded like *"Cats"*...?

The time has come for me to ascend to the cuisine and create another sumptuous repast. (We have also started up our gourmet club again—as if we need another excuse to eat and drink.) This evening's Menu is still a mystery to me, but have no fear, after a few libations to the gods, all will be revealed. If not, I'll be past caring and will have spaghetti again. In the meantime, in the crueltime, ain't we got fun!

As always,
Pete

P.S. I must say that the thought of public exposure, such as you plan, is somewhat intimidating. I am more than a little self conscious but will try to overcome this fear for the sake of a bad pun and the enlightenment of the literate world.

P.P.S. I am also working on my unvarnished autobiographical sketch for the collection of letters, missives, epistles, ruminations and astute observations in which you are so kindly including me. I have had to climb down the family tree a bit to create a view that will be a true and balanced portrait of your humble servant. Trying to maintain that delicate balance between Nurture and Nature whose confluence carries us on the course that is ourselves.

To Peter Taylor   From Jamie MacVicar   March 23, 1995

Dear Petah!

How nice to hear from you. Congratulations on your new job as curator. If anyone can discover a cure, you can. Incidentally, your cousin Matilda just left today, and I must say, I most enjoyed her company; although, having spent a week with the young lass (you trusting soul), I find it difficult to resist commenting on a social phenomenon to which I have become a part, albeit unintentionally.

Having lived here in the nation's capital almost twenty years, among some of the most opinionated folks you'd ever want to meet, it suddenly occurred to me that I and my colleagues had actually developed what can only be termed the "art of disagreement."

Since it had developed somewhat gradually, I didn't even realize I had it until last week when your cousin, who was equally opinionated, landed at my doorstep. Naturally, I included her in the Washington ritual of going out to dinner, specifically to opine on the events of the day.

Unfortunately, since our opinions crossed the political spectrum, from "Newt's right. All illegitimate children should be placed in orphanages" to "The trouble with the nation's poor is they're fed too much," my visiting friend became increasingly agitated. In fact, as calmly as we lobbed these bombs and responded in kind, we were somewhat taken aback by the heated responses of young Matilda. In fact, not only did she become white and then red in the face, but her responses escalated from, "I totally disagree!" to "Are you some kind of a bonehead? That is the stupidest thing I have ever heard."

She was perfectly right, of course, but judging from the defensiveness in which she placed my companions, it gradually dawned on me. She has no understanding of the "art of disagreement." Consequently, the next morning I took her aside and explained, "Here in Washington, the degree to which one disagrees and takes offense at the stupidity of another's remark is in direct proportion to the amount of praise you first administer."

She seemed a bit bewildered, so to use one of my earlier examples, I indicated an appropriate response might be:

A pause and then, "Gee, that's very interesting; however, might I add a divergent thought..." (This is for mild disagreement.)

- or -

"That's really insightful... although, someone might argue..."

(This is for stronger disagreement—note the deflection from oneself.)

- or -

"That's quite imaginative, I must say... however, I wonder if historians might differ with you on a point or two..." (even stronger disagreement)

- or -

"That's really ingenious. I marvel at your ability to penetrate to the core of the issue; however, if I might interject a slightly different twist to your reasoning..." (Absolute, total disagreement whereby the party of the first part is so neutralized by praise he hardly knows he's being disagreed with.)

By week's end, I must say, she had mastered the art and was parrying with the best of them. In fact, on the way to the airport, I interjected, "What the middle class needs is a good cut in the capital gains tax."

To which she replied, "A very astute observation; however, there are some that might argue..."

Sir Jamie

To Jamie MacVicar   From Fred MacVicar   April 4, 1995

Dear Sir Jamie, Pretender to the Porcelain Throne,

    I woke up this morning thinking of the honeymoon tradition. I remembered having breakfast with your mother on the morning following our first night of wedded bliss and shuddering at the forlorn look of despair and disappointment which was to remain etched on her face throughout our thirty years of marriage.

    I remembered the pitiful expression of deprivation and advanced sexual starvation on the face of your first bride immediately after your honeymoon, and how she rushed to embrace your fraternity brothers and welcome them into your intimate little family.

    I remembered your big sister's honeymoon when her new husband sold her to the Fiji Island witch doctor for six conch shells.

    I remembered the look of surprise on the face of my old pal, Barney MacDoo, when he discovered his new bride had undergone surgery in Sweden after an unsuccessful career as a bull rider.

    I remember when Bucko Donovan eloped with the bearded lady he'd met in the Halifax pub and awoke in the morning with the terrible realization that he'd wedded Sergeant Major MacPansey of the gaily-kilted Fandango Highland Regiment.

    And, I remembered the pitiful look of anguish, despair and disbelief on the face of auld "Milker" MacLeaks when he described to me how his new bride's 48-D mammaries dropped down to her ankles when she removed her burlap brassiere on their wedding night.

    At times, it's nice to reminisce.
    Your Alleged Father

To Fred MacVicar   From Jamie MacVicar   May 4, 1995

Dear Father,

    Until recently, I thought I had seen it all in the business of advertising. There was the time during the annual review of one of my employees the gentleman in question folded his arms and announced he'd be taking the Fifth Amendment from then on in. Then there was the time the spouse of one of my artists broke into our office at three in the morning via the skylight, only to discover he was dangling thirty feet above a stairwell. Nor will I forget the designer who liked to sit cross-legged under her drafting table for several minutes at a time... no one dared ask why; but suffice it to say, these minor incidents pale in my memory banks compared to a meeting I had last week in Baltimore.

    I was minding my own business, when I received a call from a prominent, elderly banker in Baltimore. I had worked with him once before several years ago and frankly found him as loony as a March hen, but since he'd been promoted to president of the bank and was in need of our services, I thought, "What the hell?"

    Well, I got to his office building, took the elevator up to the seventeenth floor and was ushered into a spacious room with panoramic views of the city. Within a few short minutes, the president (looking even more manic than the last time I saw him) strode in.

    "Jamie! Good to see you," he hollered ebulliently.

    "It's good to see you, sir," I said shaking his hand.

    "Listen," he said, changing his countenance, "I don't have time for small talk. I'll get right to the point." He then proceeded to tell me he was in need of an image campaign for his bank. I was, of course, all ears, since this is what we do, and I figured as long as he didn't bark at the moon, and we got paid, "What the hell?"

    Well, he rambled on for what seemed like several minutes until I felt it necessary to ask the obvious, "Exactly, sir, what image would you like to have?"

At which point, he leaned forward (I'm not making this up), stared me in the eye, lowered his voice and said, "I'm glad you asked, Jamie. I'll tell you what image I'd like to have... I'll tell it to you in two words," and he leaned even closer. "Religious experience."

"Pardon?" I said.

"Religious experience," he repeated. "When a customer leaves one of our branches, I want him to have had a religious experience."

My first impulse was to ask, "Would that be a Christian or Muslim experience?"

Now you can imagine how difficult it was to keep a straight face, especially when I realized he was dead serious. The thought occurred to me, we could dress him in a white robe and sandals and lower him from the rooftop at appropriate times. I almost suggested it, but I was afraid he'd love the idea. Thank God, he said something moderately funny a few minutes later, which allowed me to roll on the floor in tears for about ten minutes.

At any rate, I promised him I'd address the creative staff and get back to him next week. Help!

Lord Jamie
(no pun intended)
The esteemed Reverend Jamie
Acolyte Extraordinaire
Up the Red Sea Without a Paddle
Yuk Yuk

P.S. This could be the perfect account for you. Perhaps you could attend the next meeting astride a donkey! Perhaps your ads could be in the shape of tablets. Perhaps we could put offering plates in front of the tellers. Perhaps Charleton Heston... That's enough! I've got to collect myself before facing my creative people.

To Jamie MacVicar   From Fred MacVicar   May 8, 1995

Dear Jamie,

I have labored long and hard in the vineyards of my fertile mind and arrived at the solution to your client's "religious experience" advertising campaign "creative platform."

I've never met your client, but know at once that he is a giant of financial strategy. Only a genius would unerringly go to the heart of the far right and carve out this vital niche to the exclusion of the moderate and the far left riff-raff who now rush to deposit their paltry earnings in his prestigious financial institution. Foresight founded on insight.

He is right on target in his marketing rationale and a sure recipient of the American Banking Association's Golden Squeeze Award, if he will only adhere to the following campaign strategy:

1. Arrange for hourly hostage-taking raids by armed Muslim terrorists. Every single customer will enjoy a memorable religious experience, soil his shorts and pray incessantly.

2. Place a condom recycling bin at each teller's window and donate the proceeds to the Cub Scouts or the Campfire Girls.

3. Offer free baptism of all unborn children, dunking all pregnant mothers and toweling them down before escorting them penniless from the bank.

4. Have each branch manager provide immaculate conception free of charge for all virginal female and gay customers of child-bearing age.

Glad I could help you on this one. My best to your client. Is he a Scots Canadian or some other superior intellect?

Love,
Dad

To Fred MacVicar   From Jamie MacVicar   June 7, 1995

Dear Father,

The other day I was toying with the title, *The Advance Man*, and had an idea of adding a subhead to the title—The Adventures of a Huckster—which led me to wondering where in the world did the word "huckster" come from. My first thought was it came from Huckleberry Finn for his talents of persuasion, but upon further research, I discovered huckster came from the Dutch word "hoekster" which was a derivative of the word "hawker." A "hawker," I came to find out, was a man during medieval times who purchased falcons and birds of prey (generally from northern Europe) and resold them at county fairs to lords and nobles. He was known for his salesmanship which soon led to such expressions as "hawking his wares."

This, of course, led me to the study of falconry, who could own them and who couldn't, how they were used, etc. But at any rate, from one huckster to another, I thought you'd find this a wee bit interesting.

Love,
Jamie

P.S. This may explain why birds keep doo dooing on your car.

To Jamie MacVicar   From Fred MacVicar   June 28, 1995

Dear Odoriferous Roe of the Great Horned Mackerel,

Your brother David informs me that he's become enamored with the sport of fly fishing. Poor helpless little flies! In my experience, it's usually the lady anglers who go for the flies. Perhaps you can talk to him or get him some professional help. I've fished for aquatic creatures such as shark, trout and salmon. I've fished for fish-out-of-water such as clients and investors. I've even fished for sympathy, compliments and clues. But damned if I'd ever fish for some poor helpless little fly, casting my manure-baited hook into the swarm and hoping for a tiny nibble.

My years as a charter boat fishing captain taught me that there's one ultimate fishing experience, where skill, sportsmanship and the thrill of victory combine to pound the pulse and boil the blood.

Bottom fishing (preferably from a seaworthy houseboat anchored in a sleepy lagoon) is the pinnacle of fishing adventure. The presentation of the lure, the skillful use of the rod, the setting of the hook when one feels the strike and the rapture of catching a trophy-class bottom. Flies, marlin and tuna pale in comparison.

Talk to your little brother and extol the virtues of bottom fishing. Persuade him to abandon fruitless fly fishing pursuits. Suggest he swat or spray the little bastards. There's no meat on them, they taste like cow manure and they're too crunchy. Furthermore, baiting your hooks with manure balls can rot off your fingers.

Love, Your Alleged Spawner

P.S. If he needs bottom fishing equipment, lend him yours.

To Fred MacVicar   From Jamie MacVicar   August 10, 1995

Dear Father,

It occurred to me the other day that I never properly thanked you for the times when the three of us—Mother, you and myself—would be riding in the car together, and Mother would spot something undesirable upon my face; whereupon, she would reach into her purse, pull out a used wad of Kleenex (I knew this by the lipstick stains), "spit" on it, and then proceed to scour the aforementioned patch. Now I ask you, what on earth could possibly have been on my face worse than that?

Now what precedes this little diatribe is, not once, but more than once, I caught you bemused by this spectacle (in fact, on one occasion, you even pointed out a smudge), but just to show you how much I have matured and accept your lack of interference in this little indignity, I hereby forgive you both now and in eternity.

Love,
Jamie

P.S. I hope you haven't been holding this letter by the green ends.

P.P.S. To give Mother her fair due, she was a formidable opponent. Perhaps it was her nurse's training, but to this day, I'm not sure I could squirm out of her grasp once the wee little thing had her heart set on rendering me presentable.

To Jamie MacVicar   From Fred MacVicar   August 20, 1995

Dear Son,

Try to forgive your mother for finding something undesirable on your face. As you must realize by now, it's virtually impossible *not* to find something undesirable on your face.

With regard to the smudges, your mother is nearsighted and probably mistook your freckles for splattered doo doo. With regard to the wad of Kleenex, it was only slightly soiled, and the lipstick was intended to put roses in your little cheeks. She cleaned your little bottom with it too. The spit was to give it fragrance and provide lubrication.

I was neither bemused nor amused by the spectacle. I was in awe of your skillful whining, whimpering and sniveling and showed fatherly pride in your unbelievably high threshold of pain. Most kids would have cracked under the pressure, but you bravely withstood the agony and the tirades, screwing up your little face and pissing her off instead of faking death or unconsciousness. Your sister held her breath until she turned blue, and if that didn't work, threw up on you or the car seat or both, throwing your mother into a state of shock.

By the way, the word huckster, according to my research, comes from the Mongolian pronunciation of the word heck. Where we say, "What the heck," Mongolians say, "What the huck," "Let's get the huck out of here," or "Huck it." A huckster or hucksteress is one who hucks for a livelihood. The words huckster, hooker, lawyer and politician are synonymous.

Hope this information gets you back on track. Keep thinking.

Love,
Dad

To Peter Taylor   From Jamie MacVicar   September 1, 1995

Dear Petah!

That's it! I've had it! Once again I've been accused by a member of the opposite species of "wanting my cake and eating it too." (I wouldn't be nearly as upset if I was "having" my cake and eating it too... but I digress.)

Well, I pose this question to you. Why is it, when they talk about marriage, and I say, "You needn't worry. As long as I'm happy, I'll be here," they get upset? I'll tell you why. They want to know you'll be there regardless of whether they make you happy. Now, if that's not having your cake and eating it too, I don't know what is.

Or, as my old grand pappy used to say, "You don't need to put a fence around the dog to teach him where his food is."

Your friend,
"Woof Woof"

To Jamie MacVicar   From Pete Taylor   September 8, 1995

Dear Woof Woof,

Salutational greetings and a hearty hi ho, Phido. I always thought eating one's cake was what one was supposed to do. Why leave a tasty morsel unattended? It would be wasteful and illogical. Your friend's use of this phrase makes her suspect in my book. Obviously this sweet, toothsome wench (old English usage is still PC when used as a literary device, isn't it?) is afraid that you may go out for danish and not come back or worse.

You have arrived at your particular predicament by way of what the lexicographers term "situational and contextual incompatibility." This is the juxtapositioning of words in a thought phrase that causes the female of the species to become defensive, matrimonially aggressive or vindictively homicidal. This condition is triggered in most instances by the female mentioning the word "marriage" followed by, as in your classic case, old sayings involving possession and consumption.

At the first mention of the word "marriage," a male should not respond directly and, under no circumstances, employ a phrase such as, "as long as I am happy." What you should say is, "You make me—so happy, and I hope that I will always be able to make you happy." Now the female knows that you are happy with her and the relationship, and that you are concerned about her happiness. (Notice the use of "hope" and "always"—much better than "as long as I.") There may come a time when you are no longer happy and therefore can no longer make her happy, then you can say, "I don't feel I am making you happy..."

Of course, this approach may only work for a while, then the dreaded word reappears from beneath the calm surface of conversation, rearing its ugly head, breathing the fires of discontent. At this point, there are four tacts that one can take. 1) Say, "No, definitely out of the question." Kiss this relationship goodbye and better luck next time, Amigo. 2) "Maybe." Not an advisable route to take—clearly this path is fraught with danger and difficult explanations. 3) "Yes, but only after I see my shrink to be certified." Or, fourthly, an unqualified, "Yes, I'll marry you in a minute if...

1) You are the kind of woman who will support her husband;
2) You will be the mother of the eight little bag pipers that I have always wanted to father;
3) You will be available night or day to satisfy my voracious sexual appetite including certain sexual predilections;
4) You don't mind if I maintain my purely platonic and chummy relationship with a dozen or so intelligent, attractive and independent women with whom I play cards and go fishing;
5) You will sign a prenuptial agreement."

If she says yes to all of these things, and she likes a good whiskey and a leg of lamb with garlic—MARRY HER! and Devil take the hindmost.

In the words of the immortal Bard, "If cake be the food of Love, bake on."

As always,
Pete

To Peter Taylor   From Jamie MacVicar   September 20, 1995

Dear Peter,

Thank you for your most recent response. I must say, I have now reached a much calmer state. Fortunately, "angst and inner conflict" mixed with a bit of introspection often brings clarity and a richer understanding to issues of the heart. My last girlfriend and I often argued over "spiritual vs. material" things. Unfortunately, I was never able to define the "spiritual," even though I very well knew the warm and wonderful feelings it produced. Thanks to my latest angst, I've finally arrived at a definition of the world in which I often reside: "A spiritual world is a world in which pleasures are derived from nonmaterial things." The smell of a flower. Wheat swaying in the wind. The sound of music. A good book. Turquoise waters. A beautiful sunset. Bonding with one another. These are the pleasures of a spiritual world.

When two people, lovers of which I speak, value that world above all, and each can revel in the moment "unagendasized," an exchange of energy occurs (literally, molecules pass back and forth) that is like no other. It is warm and exhilarating and transcending. In short, it is "love."

But when both, or either one of them for that matter, enters the material world and attaches an agenda (will she love me more after sharing the sunset; will this lead to forever and ever) to the moment, then even though one might experience the beauty of the spiritual world, the "special sharing," and the "exchange of energy" that leads to such profound feelings of love for one another is cut off.

It's a strange concept, and by no means do I exclude material comforts from earthly pleasures, but if it's inner harmony one seeks, then it's a "blending" of the two I recommend. I know not much of many things, but this I know.

Your friend,
Jamie

To Jamie MacVicar   From Pete Taylor   September 22, 1995

Dear Jamie,
    Enclosed is my short autobiographical sketch, per your request, for the front of the book. Feel free to edit as you see fit.

Autobiographical Sketch on the Life and Times of Peter A. B. Taylor

    Having climbed down the family tree to see from whence I came, I am once again struck by the fact that Chance has played such a starring role in the production of yours truly as well as a great many other lesser productions. A couple meets by chance, fall in love and make love (one usually hopes that it was love, if only fleeting, and not just a meaningless bonk that brought them into this world) on a particular day when a particular egg is fertilized by a peculiar sperm and voila, raise curtain—enter actor stage right. Realizing at an early age the mechanics of Chance, I have lived my life accordingly. This accounts for my varied, some have said unstable, history. Although unpredictable, this approach to life leaves room for that odd spontaneous act that proves both enjoyable and edifying. It also provides other experiences that are not so, but all is grist for the mill.
    Where to begin this timeless chain of events? ...Great grandma! My great grandmother was a Chinese noblewoman, who after being married to an unlucky warlord, was sold into servitude and later purchased by my great grandfather, Andre Bosquet, in Manchuria and taken back to Switzerland, much to the consternation of his wife. Old Andre's lifestyle was a little more than the usual Swiss reserve could bear, so he packed up his wife, six children, Chinese consort and his Italian mistress and moved to Brussels. He settled into the import/export business and lived life the way he thought it should be lived. He fathered two more children with his Swiss wife, four by his

Italian mistress and two with my great grandmother, Wyoon Tang. By all accounts they lived amiably enough in a large residence on the Rue des Reveries.

My grandfather, the first issue of the union of Andre and Wyoon Tang, also entered the family business and prospered, eventually marrying and having a daughter, Gisele, who was my mother.

Chance would have it that my mother's best friend was the girlfriend of my father's brother when he was stationed in Belgium during WW II. He mentioned to Gisele that he had a brother stateside, and English being one of the seven languages in which she was fluent, she started a correspondence that ended in late January of 1947 when she stepped off a plane in New York with a six-week visa. Five weeks later, she and my father were married. Two years later, yours truly arrived, the second son with just a hint of my great grandmother around the eyes.

My father, on the other hand, came from old Welsh stock who settled in Chester County, Penn. in the early 1680s. Like the Bosquets, they prospered. Unfortunately, my great grandfather sold his share of the land and business and at the age of twenty-nine retired, to spend the next fifty-four years in the pursuit of, as the song says, young women, old whiskey and fast horses. His only problem was that he couldn't keep his adjectives straight. Despite this fact, he left a legacy any hedonist would be hard pressed to carry on but the family has nevertheless been trying.

The only fly in the familial ointment has been my brother, who has shirked rightful duty and after pursuing a couple of graduate degrees in Chemistry, settled down to a career in the pharmaceutical industry. Meanwhile, it was left up to me to spend my college years working on my alcohol dehydrogenates and ekeing out a degree in political science. The thought being to go into politics and cash in on the money, babes and power. But, as Chance would have it, I heard the call of the Muse and went back to school to study Art. Emerging with a diploma in one hand and a wedding ring on the other, I embarked on what might best be described as a journey. Making art, doing illustration, foundry and factory work, graphic arts production and sales, design production coordination and finally back to art. During this time, I have traveled most of North America and Europe, lived in a half-dozen places, been used for target practice, the victim of mistaken identity, drank and danced with the Gypsies in Spain, been at Death's door a time or two, desired and been the object of desire, learned to cook fairly well, read a great many books and found my passion in art and music. All the while, making a great many mistakes and increasingly becoming more comfortable with myself.

So here I am at the age of forty-six, a sculptor, living in Greensboro, NC with a wife of 23 years, a 15-year-old daughter and working as a curator for the local Artists' League. Generally speaking, I am an optimist, a lazy perfectionist and usually in good humor. I am also always on the lookout for one of Chance's "happy accidents," in life as well as in art. But unlike the young fellow of my youth, I realize that one can take actions that will encourage those accidents. Still, the trick is to recognize them when they happen.

To Jamie MacVicar   From Fred MacVicar   September 23, 1995

Dear Reasonable Facsimile Thereof,

 I was unable to sleep last night, and as I lay there tossing and turning on my bed of nails, found myself reminiscing about bygone years when you were weaned, trained and launched into society.

 Remember when your mother wouldn't let your sister shave her legs, and you called her "Monkey Legs?" What a joy you were.

 Remember when you played high school football and bottomed out with bench splinters? Inexplicably, the coach hated your guts, probably because you were hitting on his favorite cheerleader. Remember when you were crewing on the sailboat and got your belt buckle hung up in the spinnaker halyard? I had you hoisted halfway up the mainmast before I realized the mewing and screaming wasn't coming from a ruptured sea gull.

 Remember lifting weights with my friend's son, Praig, and how we laughed and laughed when the obnoxious little peckerwood dropped the weight and broke his arm? The mothers were not amused.

 The following year, you gave your little, three-year-old, barefoot sister a fast ride on the back fender of your bicycle, grinding off half her right ankle in the wheel spokes. I was not amused.

 Tossing on my bed of nails, I remembered hosting your high school graduation party, when you and your fellow ROTC officers goose stepped through the living room waving your sabers and vowing to stamp out tyranny, dictatorship, socialism and the dreaded institution of virginity. Reluctantly, I vowed to help.

 Among my fondest memories was of the beautiful summer day we spent at the beach here on Hilton Head Island. How you ran and played with the big horny dog who grew attached to your right hind leg. How hundreds of tourists cheered as he ran you down and showed his canine devotion. Animals can sense when they're loved.

Then there was the time when you worked for the weekly paper in the Shenandoah Valley and you came under attack by a flock of barn swallows, all trying to pluck you bald. It was fun to watch.

Remember when you lost a contact at the corner of Connecticut Avenue and M Street in Washington and crawled around on your hands and knees during the rush hour? The Zen Buddhists were feeding you scraps of bread when the dog catcher arrived. That was your tenth lost contact in a month, and your mother wanted to leave you in the pound. Somewhat reluctantly, I intervened.

As I finally drifted off to sleep, I remembered dragging you and your big sister all over Alaska in the banana box I'd converted to a sled. The natives all thought you were bananas.

There's a lot of other stuff I remembered, but most of it's too sordid to recount here—your numerous amorous exploits, the crash of the go cart, the great mountain bike adventures, the winter we ate Santa's reindeer, your career as an acolyte and the night your car was towed from the Black Horse Tavern, to mention only a few. Thank you for the many exciting memories.

Love,
Dad

To Fred MacVicar   From Jamie MacVicar   September 27, 1995

Dear Father,

Thanks for the remembrances. On a slightly more serious note, you forgot one—the hours we spent, just you and I (the women folk having gladly left us) watching John Wayne (remember *Red River* and *Yellow Ribbons*?), William Holden (I think we had the script of *The Bridge Over the River Kwai* memorized), Steve McQueen (*The Sand Pebbles, The Great Escape*), Gregory Peck in *The Guns of Navarone*, and my favorite, Errol Flynn (who can forget *The Wake of the Red Witch*, *Robin Hood* and of course, *Crossed Swords*?).

What do fathers and sons watch together today? It seems as though we had heros back then. They all had one thing in common. They were all "reluctant" heros. William Holden hated going back to the island, even though he was the only one that could blow up the bridge. John Wayne never wanted to leave his family, but duty called. Who else would lead a ragtag band of outcasts if Errol Flynn didn't do it, at the risk of the hangman's noose, I might add?

Thanks for sharing those characters with me. As a little boy, they were my heros, bigger than life... and so were you, and that made it very special.

By the way, there's one more... one I almost forgot. You'll remember it by a parting line you used to say to me right before I went to bed... "It's a fine thing you do, Gunga Din!"

Peace be with you.

Love,
Jamie

To Jamie MacVicar   From Fred MacVicar   October 3, 1995

Dear Jamie,

Reading some of your correspondence with Peter and perusing your letters to me, it seems to me that you are delving into the perplexities and meanings of life on earth. Perhaps I can shed a penetrating ray of light on this subject.

Throughout recorded history, the dominant message has been a chronicle of man's inhumanity to man, beast and every other living thing on the face of the earth. Somewhere, right now, another Genghis Khan, Attila the Hun, Jack The Ripper, Adolf Hitler, Thuggee, Colin Ferguson, Charles Manson, Henry the VIII, Rasputin or Boston Strangler is waiting to strike. Hundreds of warlords, terrorists, spouses and offspring are eager to wreak havoc on their fellow mankind and exact revenge for real or imagined injuries, eternal life or just plain fun.

Several centuries from now, the promise that the meek will inherit the world will wear thin. By then, the meek will rule the meeker and the meekest. A wise man will come along and give heart to the multitude for another few centuries stating unequivocally that the meekest will inherit the world. The meekers (the middle class) will always hold the middle ground. Essentially, there will be King Meek, General Meeker and Private Meekest, who's trying to work his way up to the rank of Meeker. He is the Horatio Meekest of future generations and will prevail. Meanwhile, the General Meekers will destroy the King Meeks, and a new pecking order will be established for mankind— Meekers, Meekests and Sub-Meeks. And priests and wise men shall be there to guide them and exhort them in their inhumanity to mankind. With regard to man's inhumanity to other living creatures, history is replete with examples of our wanton destruction of the earth's flora and fauna. Hundreds of species have become extinct in the few years I've lived here. Never again will I fondle a mastodon, tickle a saber-tooth tiger, ride a unicorn or stroke my dinosaur. Soon we'll lose the crocodiles, the mosquitoes, the poison ivy and the tsetse fly. We will eventually lose lawyers and bankers, eliminating the need for real money and reverting to the barter system of yesteryear, when a plucked chicken bought you twelve nice pieces of donkey and cannibalism prevented starvation.

The morals and trustworthiness of mankind also remain constant throughout recorded history. "Et tu, Brute," rings as true today as it did in Caesar's time. There will always be a Quisling, an embezzler, a slanderer and an unfaithful, overpaid mistress.

Upon our deaths, our grandchildren may have vague memories of our bad breath or unclean fingernails. Our great-grandchildren will have highly fragmented bits and pieces of bad-breath-and-dirty-fingernail stories woven into their disinterested high-tech minds. Beyond that, unless we have written a bestseller or the sequel to the Bible, left a fortune or played football, we will sink into the abyss of anonymity from which we came. All that will remain of us on this earth will be poisonous weeds growing from our left-behind fertilizer and doomed to ruthless eradication by future generations of uncaring mankind.

The ancient Greeks believed that a man remains alive as long as his memory remains alive on earth. Hence "tombstones?" With regard to living a balanced life or a "full" life, there appear to be different strokes for different folks. All of us seem to apply different weights to different aspects of our lives. Some like solitude, others like crowds. Some like to experience adventures, others like to read about them. Some of us like to live on the edge, others like it in the middle. Dad worked for one company all of his life. I'd have gone mad. I know many more happy bums than I know happy bankers. Weird?

I think one of the things about homo sapiens that's so perfectly obvious, yet so widely ignored, is that man changes from minute to minute throughout his entire life. We are not the same men today as we were yesterday—or even now as we were just a moment ago. Every second we are bombarded with new impressions, values, experiences and impulses. A chance encounter can change our lives forever. A word, a book, a person, a place or a glance will immediately change us, yet we expect others to remain ever constant and unchanged. I once thought that sex was the most satisfying physical pleasure in life, until I experienced the long-awaited relief from a prolonged period of constipation.

As you know, I have partaken eagerly of life's challenges, joys, experiences and adventures. And through storytellers and books, I have shared in the experiences, conquests, fortunes and misadventures of thousands of others. And it's been fun.

I have had both happy and unhappy relationships with the men and women I've met in my lifetime, including the meek, the meeker and the meekest. There are even first-class sons-of-bitches who have enriched my life more than many I even loved. If you live to be 100 years old, which you undoubtedly will, and urinate five times daily for an average time of five minutes per leak, you will urinate for 15,208 hours or approximately two years of your life. That's enough of your life to piss away.

I think there's at least one grain of truth in every single thing I've ever been told or read. The problem is to find the grain. On the other hand, if it makes me happy, does it make a damn? I've noticed that everything with which I agree is almost invariably true, so I suspect that I'm an extremely wise man.

As you must know, you've been a very big piece of my goodly slice of a very full life, laddie buck. Keep on keeping on!

Love,
Dad

To Peter Taylor   From Jamie MacVicar   October 10, 1995

Dear Peter,

It slowly occurred to me over the last two or three weeks, thanks to a silly putty relationship I'm having with my last letter to you, that I can't quite let go of it until I've focused a little more strongly on one particularly important concept. You may recall my use of the term "blending" to which I philosophically ascribed. Well, despite its off-the-cuff veracity, the reason I can't let go of the word is, unfortunately, it conflicts with a cultural phenomenon that has taken me more than a few years to reconcile. Now I've touched on this phenomenon before, but since, for me, it seems so incredibly simple yet so difficult to attain and so impacting on our thinking, I thought I must elaborate a little further.

The fact of the matter is, we as Americans, for this is definitely a part of our culture, don't deal in nuances, subtleties, or shades of grays. Instead, our immediate response to most situations is, "Is it yes or no? Are you with me or against me? Is it black or white? Are you in or out?"

This, as Herb Cohen, a well-known negotiator would point out, plays havoc when our State Department finds itself negotiating with a society that more readily sees the in-betweens. Then again, they may not have grown up the way we have. Even our movies are quick to point out the good guy vs. the bad guy; who's right and who's wrong. It's the American way!

The problem is, life doesn't work that way. If I've learned anything, and I must say it takes continuous conscientious effort, it's that life is a matter of "blending," especially in "relationships." It's perfectly o.k. to realize I love this in this person, but I don't like that. It doesn't have to be "all" or "none."

"Well, if that's the case," someone might say, "how in the world do you evaluate the relationship?"

The answer is, "It's easy. It's a matter of balance. If the balance is 80/20, then maybe that's acceptable. If the balance is 50/50, then maybe it isn't."

But it's not just love relationships. I can't tell you how many other dichotomies I have wrestled with. Do I yearn for a small-town life or big-city excitement? Is it hearth and home I want or unbridled freedom? Would I rather work and get ahead or sip cafe on the Cote D'Azur? The truth is, I want all of these things, but as a wise ol' sage finally pointed out to me, it's not "either/or," "all or none," "black and white," it's a "blending" of the two. Live in the city while escaping to the country; find a mutually loving, nurturing relationship but maintain your sense of self; work and accomplish things but take time to enjoy life's simple pleasures. It's the "blending" that leads to harmony. How much blending is a matter of balance.

Well, there it is, kind sir. A simple but sometimes soothing insight I had to bring to conclusion. I hope you'll forgive me, and I hope all is well. Write soon.

Sir Jamie

To Peter Taylor   From Jamie MacVicar   October 25, 1995

Dear Pete,

    I just returned from nine glorious days in the Caribbean—Turks Caicos this time. I can still feel the cool balmy breezes upon my skin and smell the scent of cocoa butter, if I close my eyes and activate my senses. Travel, I've decided is something I cannot not do. It's not just the chance to revel in new experiences but more importantly, to reflect on my life from afar.

    Incidentally, my father invited you and me down to Hilton Head. He seems to think you'd like one another. I happen to agree. As for me, my father and I always had a love/hate relationship. The first twenty years, I loved him and he hated me. The next twenty years, he loved me and I hated him. The last four years, we've been circling one another, "blending" I suppose. I guess that's when we started writing each other. I suppose it's the closest we've ever been. A man once said of another, "I've nothing to give him anymore, at least nothing he would take, so I give him humor. I can at least make him laugh. It's a gift he can't give back." He was right about that.

    My father never was much for compliments. As a result, I spent a lot of time trying to please him. He lost his own father about five years ago. He was deeply affected, but I remember most clearly his saying, "Suddenly, I feel cut adrift." A little later, he struck up a friendship with a fellow named Charlie. I met Charlie the last time I visited my father. I was struck by how much Charlie reminded me of my father's father.

    Well, anyway, to make a long story short, I remember when I told my father I'd saved all our letters, and I wanted to put them into a book. "You did?" he said. "Why'd you do that?"

    "I don't know," I said. "It just seemed like a good idea. Would you like me to send you a copy?"

    "Yes," he said, and then he paused for a minute and gave me the biggest compliment of all, "Could you send two? I'd like

to give one to Charlie."
That pleased me. It pleased me a lot.

Take care,
Jamie

THUS ENDS, AT LEAST TEMPORARILY, THE CORRESPONDENCE BETWEEN MY FATHER, PETE TAYLOR, AND MYSELF, WITH THE EXCEPTION OF ONE FINAL MISSIVE FROM ME TO MY FATHER.

Dear Dad,
    Well, it's time to find an agent. I've selected about a hundred pages of letters. Not very long, I suppose, but then again, how much bullshit can one eat in one sitting.
    By the way, the odds of finding an agent are nil and none. I've perused our letters, and we've systematically poked fun at bankers, lawyers, females of all persuasion, charcoal grillers, Brits, nuns, and, thank God, not least of all, ourselves.
    Our only hope is a one-legged Australian.

    Best of love,
    Sir Jamie

P.S. Forget that! Pete just told me they're hopeless romantics, incurable hedonists, beer swilling storytellers. On second thought...